Geordie,

I WOULD BE VERY GRATEFUL FOR
ANY HELP FROM YOU WITH MY CANCER
CAMPAIGN.

STORY OF A 60s DRUMMER

Love **Charlie**

Charli‹

Spiderwize
Remus House
Coltsfoot Drive
Woodston
Peterborough
PE2 9BF

www.spiderwize.com

A CIP catalogue record for this book is available from the British Library.

The views expressed in this work are solely those of the author and do not necessarily reflect the views of the publisher, and the publisher hereby disclaims any responsibility for them.

ISBN: 978-1-911596-67-7

*This book is dedicated to my
wonderful grandchildren,
EMILY, BEN, ROSIE, SAM, FINLAY*

After I have recouped all my initial costs
of producing this book for publication,
half of my royalties will be shared
between the following cancer groups:

'Second Chancers Head & Neck
Cancer Support Group'

&

'Shout At Cancer'
(Laryngectomy Charity Group)

STORY OF A 60s DRUMMER

This the biography of a wee boy from a family in Glasgow, Scotland who grew up to experience the dream of appearing with the legendary Jimmy Page (Led Zeppelin) on Cartoone's debut album, signing to the famous Atlantic Record label, and touring the USA in support of Led Zeppelin and other great bands. Never in his wildest dreams would he have believed that he would share the stage with the best drummer in the world, John Bonham, plus Robert Plant, Jimmy Page and John Paul Jones, when Zeppelin were just starting out and trying to break America. That is what most musicians hope to achieve, but most never do.

And then tragedy struck...

CONTENTS

Foreword

It was 4.30 p.m. on Wednesday 21st April 2002, and I was in my consultant Mr Robert Sudderick's office. Robert is a brilliant top ENT surgeon. He has just told my wife Jackie and I that the lump he had taken out of my neck had cancer cells in it. He said that they were still looking for the 'Primary Cancer' (the one that caused all the trouble) and said that my immune system may have killed it off, but they would still keep looking every month, as it often hides itself for up to two years before showing itself. We were both stunned and shocked at the same time, as I couldn't understand. Why me? I had never smoked or abused my body in any way. In fact, I have always been very fit, so what brought this on? It's the last thing we would have expected to hear.

Mr Sudderick said it was just bad luck, as he really couldn't give me an answer on the cause of this devastating news. There are numerous reasons connected to the causes of cancer. Stress, diet, hereditary, too much sun, radiation and overuse of mobile phones are just some of the theories out there. He then told me that I would have to undergo eight weeks of daily radiotherapy under another consultant top oncologist Dr. Stephen Whitaker. I was in the best hands possible as both men are at the top of their respective fields, but still I found it all too much to take in. I felt angry, sad, numb with shock, all at the same time. Who wouldn't? Cancer is an ugly scary word!

But with the help and support of my wife Jackie and my three sons and their families, I managed to accept that it was for the best in the long term. It wasn't going to cure itself that was for sure. After finishing the radiotherapy my consultant then told me I would have to undergo another operation to take out my 'lymph glands' as a preventative measure. Apparently that's how the cancer travels, through the lymph nodes. Reluctantly, but not having much choice, I had this operation on 11th September 2002 which left me with a 12 inch scar running from behind my right ear down to the front of my throat, all held together very nicely with giant staples. Thankfully, all the lymph glands that were taken out were clear of any cancer. I had a joke with Mr Sudderick to put them back as they were clear. Hopefully, that will be the last of the treatments I have to endure.

All this got me thinking about facing the fact that I could die from this horrible illness (hopefully not). Believe me, when you face death, it makes you appreciate life much more, as you realise how precious your life is, and how important family and friends are to you. I have a wonderful loving family and friends, that's what I treasure and appreciate the most.

My wife, Jackie, the light of my life, is so gorgeous and warm and I'm so bloody lucky to have met and married such a wonderful woman. We have had a fantastic life together, full of ups and downs as that is life, but hopefully we will have many more years together to enjoy. As I know that I'm now living on borrowed time.

As I faced the possibility of dying, I started to look back over my life and what, if anything, I had achieved. I began to get the idea that I must write it all down while my memory was still working so my three sons would know what their old dad got up to when he was a young. Also, my beautiful grandchildren will be able to read it when they grow up and maybe know their grandad a bit better than they do now as children.

I must apologise to anyone who I forget to mention, as I'm writing this as a 70-year-old man who never kept a diary, so it's all down to my memory, which is clear on some things and foggy on others.

Here is my story so far. Hope you enjoy it.

Chapter 1

The Glasgow Years

I was born in a small, three bedroom flat in Ashvale Row, Railway Cottages, Springburn, Glasgow. I never had a cot, I used to sleep in one of the drawers from the dresser. I share the same birthday as Sir Sean Connery and now I'm also bald with a moustache, but that's where the resemblance ends. What must it be like to be Sean Connery, over 6ft 3in tall, when you walk into a room full of people and they all gasp in awe of your very presence (not only women but the men too). That must feel fantastic to have that effect on people. Wow! No wonder these big stars have such massive egos. Who can really blame them?

Where I lived in Glasgow it was a very close community, with everyone in the neighbourhood knowing each other's business, nothing could be kept secret for long, as all the gossip was spread at the speed of light. In those days everyone left their doors open, as they didn't have such things as burglary in those communities, as everyone looked out for each other. Plus we didn't have much in the way of possessions, so there wasn't any property of worth to steal anyway.

We all lived with my grandad in his flat. It had an outside toilet, and we had to bathe in a tin bathtub in front of the fire. When I was very young, we didn't have electricity, but every house had a gaslight. It was very grim but, as everybody had the same, we didn't know any better, and we treated it as normal. I do remember that it was a happy early childhood. My mum, Dorothy, I remember, was a really beautiful young woman, and Dad, Charlie Snr, was the Tony Curtis type with a rugged handsome swarthy look .

My mum came from Birkenhead near Liverpool, and my dad came from Glasgow, so really I'm half Scottish and half Liverpudlian. I think that's great because I loved all the Beatles, Gerry and the Pacemakers, Searchers etc. so it felt nice to be associated with those great bands. But I was brought up on Irn-Bru, and you can't get any more Scottish than that.

My mum took me to Liverpool to meet her family, but sadly I don't remember when, and I have forgotten what my mum's family look like, it's so long ago, and I don't have any photos of them either to jog my memory.

Both my mum and dad seemed to get along okay at the time. I was in my own little world of football and music. I was particularly mad on football and wanted to be like Denis Law, who was my hero at the time and played for Manchester United/Scotland, so I was mostly not aware of anything happening that didn't directly concern me.

Imagine how exciting it was when everyone changed from having grim gaslight to the new and exciting 'electricity' in Scotland in the 1960s. Wow, it was amazing. The room was lit up so bright. We had a new radio (posh for us) and I used to love listening to Radio Luxemburg. Then my dad managed to scrape together the money to buy/rent a small portable TV. I remember Champion the Wonder Horse and the Lone Ranger with his sidekick Tonto. Later on, we saw that more programmes were added like *I Love Lucy* with Lucille Ball and hubby Desi Arnaz. Bruce Forsyth and *Sunday Night at the London Palladium* with the great Ronnie Verrell on drums. Everything was in black and white, no colour TV yet, but with all these new amazing things to enjoy. Life wasn't so bad really.

It was totally fantastic when we first got these wondrous things called TV and electricity. Now at this present day we are so used to it we just take everything for granted with our iPads and iPhones etc., we are so spoilt with all this new technology we don't appreciate what it was like in those days before electricity.

I remember in the 60s watching The Beatles on TV play 'live' on the Royal Variety Performance at the London Palladium, when John Lennon said the famous words 'the people at the back clap your hands, those at the front rattle your jewellery'. It was so amazing to see and hear The Beatles for the first time. It's not the same looking back now and watching in the present day. It was so new, different and exciting then – never been seen or heard before. It was the catalyst for all the music that came from Liverpool and Manchester and the rest of the country at the time in the 60s.

My grandad was a wonderful accordion player and used to play at all the parties and sing-songs we had in our house. He had a beautiful touch on the keyboard, as he made it sound so sweet. I remember that there were so many good chanters (singers) at the parties, and I loved listening to all the old songs like 'Over The Rainbow' and 'True Love' to name but a couple. My favourite was 'Tears For Souvenirs' which sounded beautiful on his accordion. Plus he was great at the old Scottish jigs, and got us all up dancing. I never smoked, but the room was so thick with smoke you didn't need too, you just breathed it in.

The first time I heard Elvis Presley was when I was walking past a cafe in Springburn, Glasgow, and I heard this wonderful voice coming out of the jukebox. The band sounded fantastic on the track. I later found out it was 'Jailhouse Rock'. I had never heard music like that before. I was used to all the pop stuff like Johnny Ray and FrankieVaughan. Elvis was so exciting and original. I was about ten years old at the time, but after hearing Elvis I was hooked on his music forever.

Elvis definitely deserved the title the King of Rock-N-Roll as he was unique. There was nobody like Elvis Presley. I followed his career after that and watched all his cheesy films over the years (some were really awful). My favourites, *GI Blues*, *Follow That Dream*, and *Loving You,* were the best and most enjoyable. Elvis was an amazing singer and performer. He was only 42 yrs old when he died in

1977. So young for someone so talented, but what a fantastic life he had.

I remember when we moved to a brand new estate called Castlemilk it was lovely to be in our own brand new house for a change, with a nice garden. Opposite our house, there was a big wood where all the kids from around the estate used to play. I really enjoyed Castlemilk with all its nice clean houses and big roads around the estate. We lived there for about three or four years. After a year, I don't know why, but my dad just up and left us. We were destitute and starving, as he didn't tell us where he was or send us any money to live. We lived on bread and dripping for a while, and my mum made stews which lasted a couple of days. I managed to get a job in December delivering milk. Wearing shorts, as I couldn't afford long trousers, and hobnail boots I delivered milk in the deep snow at 4.30 a.m. every morning; it was bloody freezing, but I must admit it did toughen me up a bit, and taught me that I would need to be determined if I wanted to get on in life. I also got a job doing the rounds with the 'Roll-Man' at night after school. At least with my mum's little job this gave us some money to live on, so at least we could eat a proper meal every day and weren't starving anymore.

About two years later, I came back from the Roll Round one night, and walked into the house, and there was my dad. Not a word in two years, and there he was as if nothing had happened. Apparently he was working in one of the big hotels in London as a Head Waiter, and returned with a posh suit on and loads of cash in his pocket. Of course my mum took him back. What else could she do? We were skint and barely scraping a living each week. I was about 12 years old then and never really knew my dad, as he was never there, other than coming in drunk with his friends, or going off to work in the morning. He seemed a strange selfish man, who put himself before his family. Sadly I never did connect with him. I don't know why as we never spoke, other than when he told me what to do. A bit sad really.

Looking back now, it's amazing how time passes without you realising it. So many of my memories have slipped away with time. I never kept a diary, so some memories are really vivid, some very vague. Apologies to anyone who I miss out or fail to mention in this story.

Growing up in Glasgow was a mixture of excitement and fear; the people were very friendly, generous, and great party givers who loved to enjoy themselves to the full, and would give you their last penny if you needed it. There were some fantastic street parties with a real band playing, and everyone literally dancing in the street. All the children used to watch from the windows of their houses, looking down at all their mums and dads enjoying themselves. Especially at Hogmanay which is renowned for its ritual and superstitious merriment.

I always looked forward to Hogmanay, as my mum and dad used to go through all the trouble to decorate the whole house so that it would be all sparkling to bring in the New Year. The saying was 'Out with the Auld, and in with the New'. We wouldn't eat all day, then the whole family would sit down after midnight to a full meal with meat and two veg, plus pudding. I was starving so I managed to eat it all anyway. When you are growing up, these traditions are great and you look forward to them and enjoy them each year.

But the darker side of Glasgow will always haunt me, as most weekends where I lived you would hear the sound of women screaming as their husbands beat them up, or a family fighting among themselves, all fueled by alcohol. The sound of the screams, you would think the woman was being murdered, but when the Police arrived, both husband and wife would turn against them, with the wife shouting 'Don't you touch my man'. I will never understand that type of loyalty. But I suppose love is blind sometimes, and family loyalty was paramount in Glasgow, so it's us against them when the 'Polis' are involved. It was pretty grim, but you managed to keep your spirits up because you always remained optimistic that life would get better in the future.

All the men in my family were alcoholics who were in denial. The saying was, 'Who me! I can do without a drink no problem!', but once they started there was no stopping until they were either sick, had picked a fight, or had passed out cold, whichever came first.

I don't know how my mum put up with my dad. She used to take the brunt of all my dad's frustrations. He would hit her for any excuse: the dinner was too hot or too cold, there wasn't enough dinner, or the steak was too small. You name it he would use it to pick on my poor mum. We used to wait until we heard him coming up the road singing (we knew he was in a good mood then), or if he came in the door quietly we were in trouble as he was definitely in a bad mood.

I remember one night in particular, I was about 16 or 17 at the time, he came in the door at midnight demanding his dinner. My mum had it ready within half an hour, as she knew what to expect. He sat down at the table to eat his dinner at about 12.45 a.m. and turned the radio up so it was blaring. Mum then turned it down as she said she was worried about the neighbours. The next thing he has got my mum by the throat saying, 'It's ma hoose, an ah can do what I please woman.'

I then lost my temper and turned the radio up again and sat in my chair saying, 'There! Are you happy now, it's loud again.' My dad let go of my mum and came over to where I was sitting, he looked down on me as I kept my gaze to the floor.

'So you think you're a hard man then' he said. I just looked up at him and said 'No'. With that he punched me full in the face, but for some reason I didn't feel it. I just lost it as I grabbed my dad by the waist, lifted him up and threw him against the wall. I then grabbed him once again and hung him by his collar on the hook behind the door. I don't know where I got the strength from. The sight of him hanging there is funny now, but it wasn't then.

He was choking! I was so raging angry, all the years that I had put up with his crap, but I told him that I would let him down if he calmed down. He nodded he would, so I let him down, then as usual all the tears of remorse came out: he didn't mean to hurt my mum, it was the drink, blah blah and so on, until the next time. But this was the first time ever that I had retaliated when he hit me.

I think I'd had enough of all the years of him drinking and then beating my mum up for no reason other than he felt like it: a typical bully.

I shouldn't speak of my dad in this way as he passed away many years ago, but under the influence of the drink he was a nasty piece of work who took all his frustrations out on his family. When he was sober, he could be a very reasonable, even likeable man.

The streets in Glasgow were full of 'Teddy Boys' standing on the corners, waiting to pick a fight with a passerby. The use of razors was commonplace, and to have a scar from a fight was seen as a badge of honour. I used to know most of the gangs around my area. Thankfully though, I wasn't part of any gang I was well liked by all the different gang members. I used to make them laugh so therefore I was left alone.

I haven't been back to Glasgow for over 50 years, as I don't have any family left alive there, so no reason to go. Hopefully, it has changed for the better, as I thought the jobs were thin on the ground, and the wages were very low. £5 a day for working from 9–5, Monday–Friday. Absolute robbery. £5 for an eight hour day (one hour for lunch). The wages were much higher in London, and there was more work around if you were willing to do it. So much was happening in London, especially with the music scene. Every pub you went into there was a live band playing. It was a really exciting place to be in the 60s, as all the music and fashion was fresh and new, and the music scene was awesome with new bands popping up every day in the clubs and in the charts.

I yearned to go to swinging London, but the opportunity never presented itself at the time.

CHAPTER 2

How I Caught the Drumming Bug

My interest in the drums began when I started going with my dad and helping him to carry his drums. Nobody owned a van in those days, except shopkeepers and tradesmen etc. We were mostly broke at the time, so we carried his black and chrome Premier drums on the bus to the gig. Funny, in all that time, he never passed on any tips or words of advice about drumming or anything else. He mostly kept his thoughts to himself. We would just travel around in silence, except for the odd grunt here and there, very sad really.

It was another world watching my dad playing in his band. They played mostly Glen Miller and Frank Sinatra tunes with a couple of jazz standards thrown in the mix. My dad used to pawn his suit on a Monday then get it out on the Friday, ready for the weekend gigs.

After seeing the film *Drum Crazy* with Sal Mineo

playing Gene Krupa, I knew then that this was what I wanted to be: a drummer. I fell in love with the drums, and even loved the look and the sound of them. I used to go and look at this beautiful silver sparkle 'Ludwig' Super Classic kit in the window of McCormacks music shop in Glasgow, yearning for the day when I could afford to buy it. I began to practice on my own, playing with a couple of drumsticks while listening to the radio. I really enjoyed it and found that I had a natural feel for the drums.

After about a year of practicing, I got my first opportunity to play the drums for real with a band. My dad's band was booked to play a wedding reception and, as usual, I came along to help carry the drums. After the wedding cake was cut by the bride and groom, the band were given loads of drinks to celebrate. My dad took a lot more than his fair share and became really drunk.

The next minute he fell from his drum stool and lay there on the floor at the back of the stage absolutely out of it. I felt really embarrassed for him.

The trumpet player told me to get behind the kit and start to play. I did this without thinking, and before I knew it, I was playing my first gig with a band. I learnt then what a difference it is from listening in the audience to being part of the sound that is produced by the band: there is no comparison really, as you have to think ahead and be aware of what you're playing, as it affects the whole sound of the band.

I also became aware very quickly, what was meant by 'light and shade' in musical terms, especially as it was an acoustic band with double bass and a brass section. The trumpet player signalled to me when to play loud, and to come down on the quiet parts. I finished the gig with my dad lying asleep behind me with a big smile on his face. I felt thoroughly embarrassed by him.

But secretly, I really enjoyed the pleasure of playing the actual drums in a proper band, rather than me playing along to Radio Luxemburg on the arm of our settee with just a pair of sticks.

I then started to save up for my own drum kit, doing odd jobs just to make a bit of money, such as milk and paper rounds. It took me almost a year to save the £30 for my first 'Broadway Drum Kit'. It was blue sparkle, and to me it was the best kit in the world, because it was mine, paid for from my hard earned money. My first ever band was a Shadows copy group called Tommy & The G Squad with my old school mate, Kenny McCadden. We used to attend Colston School in Bishopbriggs, and that's where we met and formed the group. We could do a passable 'Apache' and after about six months of that, I joined a Country &Western group called The Texans (really naff names). I then started to play with visiting singers from abroad (it was cheaper for them to do this than bring their own band).

I played with this band from Liverpool called The Undertakers and got my first taste of playing the twelve-bar blues and a few Chuck Berry songs. Wow, I thought it was great music – really exciting to play. We did a gig in a place called The Crypt, an old refurbished church, and the club was in the roof with a clever use of the space. You came in through the door and the bar was to your left. There were stairs on either side leading down to the dance floor and the stage where the band played. So the people at the bar could look down at the band playing and everyone dancing. Quite a good sound as I remember.

Anyway, there was some trouble at the bar, and the next thing I know, someone had jumped on top of me from the bar and started to punch me in the face for no apparent reason. All hell broke loose with everyone fighting, women were screaming, and the band was left to defend the stage area and our gear. What a crap ending to a perfectly good night. Why can't people just come along and have a great time, enjoy the music without all this aggro? I learned later that it was over this bloke trying to kiss someone else's girlfriend, and the boyfriend didn't like it, and it all just exploded from there with everyone involved in the end. I still don't know why he picked me to jump on though. Maybe he just didn't like drummers .

I made friends with a band called 'the Hi-Fi-Combo' which had the Sneddon brothers, Dick and Andy. They were both really funny guys. We used to have such a laugh. They used to dress really strangely onstage. They had these very weird suits made for them, with flared trousers and frilly shirts. They looked like different versions of 'Rabbie Burns' and took the Mickey out of each other something rotten. Hilarious!

My fondest memories of them will always be of us laughing till it hurt sometimes. All the members of that band had a great sense of humour. They saw the funny side to everything.

Even their manager, Danny, and the Roadie, Big John, had a brilliant sense of humour. They all had these faces that you just looked at and it made you want to laugh, mainly cause as people they didn't take themselves too seriously. Great times I will never forget.

When I was asked to join The Chevlons, my drums were in the pawn, so Mike Allison and the band paid to get them out so I could play with them – really nice of them to do that for me. Derek had already left the band a couple of years ago and was living in London with his wife and child.

We played at Aberdeen University's Students Ball in 1966. The reason I remember this, was the headline band, whose name escapes me, had a very sick drummer, so they asked me if I would play with them too. So there I was, playing the first set with The Chevlons (4 part harmony stuff) and then I just stayed at the kit when the headline band came on (no rehearsal) and did their first set (mainly they were a copy of The Who) so I was trying to be Keith Moon with them and thrash the kit, then my own band came on and I was back to a more subtle style of drumming. I must say, even though it was really exhausting, I enjoyed playing with both types of band because they were so totally different.

Another band around at that time in Scotland was Dream Police fronted by Hamish Stuart. They were a superb outfit, and I thought they played the best music and had the best singer in Scotland. Hamish's version of the song 'Walk On By' was outstanding, and the highlight of the band's performance. Hamish went on to join the world famous Average White Band in 1973. They also signed to Atlantic Records, making them the second all-Scottish band to be signed by Atlantic (Cartoone were the first) with their first debut album AWB going to number one in the USA and UK.

Their single, 'Pick Up The Pieces', went to number one worldwide and is still played in numerous films and TV adverts to this present day. Hamish co-wrote/sung some classic songs which still hold up against present music. AWB achieved ten world platinum albums and sold millions of records. AWB were one of the greatest bands ever to come out of Scotland in my opinion. I still love Hamish's solo stuff.

Steve Ferrone and the late great Robbie McIntosh, the AWB original drummers,will always be two of my all time favourite drummers.

The Pathfinders were a really loud, hugely popular, exciting band doing covers of Tamla-Motown hits. They were fronted by a character called Ian Clews (Mr Personality). Most people loved Ian, who was a Joe Cocker croaky voice type of singer. I always enjoyed their sets. They were so loud, but at the same time-exciting to listen too. Their drummer was Tim Donaldson (lovely guy).

Marmalade were the top Scottish band around at that time, with a couple of hits under their belts. There were so many excellent bands around, and the standard of the music was absolutely superb. Another great band, with a member who would later join the AWB, was The Poets (Onnie McIntyre on guitar). They did what everyone did at that time, but they disappeared for about three months and came back to the Picasso Club and blew us all away with their new songs, and also the standard of musicianship in the band had risen tremendously. Very impressive and worth all the time rehearsing they had obviously put in.

So as you can see, the place was alive with loads of great bands. 1963 to 1969 were the best years for new music with great groups like The Beatles, The

Hollies, The Rolling Stones, Chuck Berry, and The Shadows who were the UK's first real four piece guitar/bass/rhythm/drums group.

Hank Marvin had the very first Fender Stratocaster Guitar in the UK. Cliff Richard brought it back from USA for him and it gave Hank a great unique sound at the time. I liked Tony Meehan on drums but I much preferred the style of drummer Brian Bennett. I thought he was great. But as my own musical tastes developed, I got into James Brown, Marvin Gaye, Solomon Burke, Otis Redding, Sam & Dave, and the wonderful Little Stevie Wonder who would later become a legend in his own time.

All the bands were playing/writing the pop stuff in the hope of being signed to a record label, but everyone was listening to Tamla-Motown, Stax/Atlantic records which most of the clubs in Glasgow, Scotland were playing. I used to love going to the Club Picasso where all the musicians would hang out after their gigs. The atmosphere was fantastic. It had a great vibe of excitement. My favourite track they used to play was 'Ain't Too Proud To Beg' by The Temptations. It sounded so good over the house system. As you walked up the stairs, you could hear that first line of the song, 'I know you wanna leave me', and that great drum-break as the Temptations burst into song. It put everyone in a great mood, just enjoying the vibe and the music after coming back from a gig.

Everything you heard was so fresh and original from all the acts that were around at that time. You knew you were hearing it for the first time. The Beatles were amazing with their brilliant songs from the pen of Lennon & McCartney. So many excellent songs to choose from, you were spoilt for choice. It was great coming back from the gig to the Picasso to feel the buzz from the place: all these different bands with new ideas, and new music, and fashions etc. It was such a fantastic time to be in a band. You felt part of a new revolution of music.

I remember one night in particular, we (The Chevlons) were driving back from a gig in Ayrshire. It was about 2.30 a.m. and we often used to sing in the van to pass the time and to practice our harmonies. Anyway, there we were driving through Glasgow in our little Bedford Van with our manager Gordon Allison (Mike's dad) singing and playing away, when all of a sudden we were surrounded by three police cars, and had to stop for fear of hitting them. The doors were flung open, and we were told to all get out of the van. We asked 'what for?' We were told to shut up and do as they said, obviously. Who was going to argue with the Glasgow Police? Not us, that's for sure!

We obliged by getting out of the van in the knowledge that we had done nothing wrong. They pushed us up against the van, put our hands behind our backs, except for old Gordon Allison, who kept insisting there must be some mistake. 'We are a Pop Group just returning from a gig and not up to any mischief!'

The policeman said he would let us off with a caution. What a joke! This is Glasgow, where murders and beatings occur on a regular basis, people are disfigured daily by thugs taking a razor to their face. To walk the streets at night is to risk life and limb. Was it a quiet night for the Police so they thought 'let's give this lot the fright of their lives for a laugh'? Who knows. Over the top or what?

Another night, I think it was in 1966, I was 19 years old and The Chevlons were playing Paisley Town Hall. The drummer from Marmalade, wee Dougie Henderson, and I decided to go out for a fish and chip supper. I was wearing a white jacket and Dougie a black leather jacket.

We had just come around the outside of the Town Hall and gone round the corner onto the main road in Paisley, when this coach drew up beside us and all these blokes got off. Dougie and I, being friendly chaps, smiled at them as they got off the coach.

As a crowd of them got off, one of the blokes approached Dougie and asked where he came from. Before he could open his mouth to speak, this guy head butted (a 'Jock-Kiss') Dougie and made his nose bleed.

I then came forward to help, and got punched in the face by two blokes who said they were 'The Tongs from Glasgow, and had come to sort out these Paisley B******s'. I tried to tell them we were both from Glasgow, but they didn't listen, just carried on punching and kicking us. I don't know how it happened, but I managed to grab Dougie and tried to make a run for it. We were doing really well running from the line of guys waiting to have a go at us, until I saw this 'Bowie Knife' in this guy's hand.

Without thinking I just reacted and pulled Dougie onto the main dual carriageway. Lucky for us there wasn't any traffic at the time. We had managed to reach the centre of the carriageway when I saw this house-brick hit Dougie in the back, and he fell down. I then looked up behind me and saw this bottle coming down on me. I turned my head away from it, and at the same time I heard them all cheering as the bottle hit my head. A woman across the road was screaming for someone to help us, but no one did.

The Tongs all ran off and left us there in the middle of the dual carriageway, with a load of blood pouring out of my head wound onto my white jacket (not a pretty sight). I managed to stem the flow with my handkerchief and scarf, and asked Dougie, 'Are you okay?' He said that he felt sore but was not too bad considering.

'Right we are still going for the fish and chips,' I said, determined to at least get something out of this. Dougie followed me to the Chippy's, which wasn't very far and, as we entered, the woman said, 'Oh my god, what happened?'

We told her and she gave us our fish and chip supper free.

As we were walking back, eating our fish and chips, who arrived on the scene: the Police (about a half-hour too late). We told them what happened, and they escorted us safely back to the Town Hall.

We both still played our gigs that night (the show must go on etc.) and thankfully never met up with the Tongs again.

I managed to buy the 'Ludwig Super Classic' drum kit that I was always yearning for. It wasn't the silver sparkle but the blue marine pearl which was nice too. When I played it, I was amazed at the difference in quality of sound compared to my old Premier kit. It was a completely gorgeous sound, especially the Bass Drum and the Snare Drum. It just had that 'Ludwig' sound to it. Unmistakable! Even on records you could recognise it because it had a distinct sound all of its own. I loved it to bits – what a kit, awesome.

On saying that though, The Chevlons were supporting The Hollies (I can't remember where but I do remember that it was a large hall with a big stage).We set our kit up in front of The Hollies' gear, as we were opening up first. My kit was directly in front of Bobby Elliot's (drummer) and I was tuning my kit and generally messing around playing various rhythms on different drums. On hearing my Ludwig kit, I felt particularly proud.

I noticed that Bobby had a new silver sparkle Ludwig Super Classic kit which looked really nice, the one I used to crave after in McCormacks. After a couple of minutes, Bobby came out and introduced himself and had a go on my kit. Then he got behind his kit and started to do a few rhythms on it. It sounded amazing, much better than my Ludwig. I asked him why, and he told me his Ludwig kit was specially custom made to his specifications and design, that's why it sounded so good. It brought me down to earth and stopped me thinking that I had a better kit than Bobby.

I was always impressed by watching how other drummers played their kits and how they were all different. I can remember The Chevlons supporting Cat Stevens in Perth Town Hall and session drummer, Ainsley Dunbar, played my kit. He made it sound fantastic: just the way he hit the kit, he knew how to get the best out of the drums, and really grooved the band in a great version of 'Mellow Yellow'. I was very much impressed and, once again, I learned something new from another drummer: how to hit the kit properly and get the maximum sound out of it using your wrists and not your arms.

Cat Stevens was every inch the Pop-Star, immaculate in his red silk shirt and black velvet suit, and with a thick mane of black hair which was really shiny. He began really well, bringing out all his hits like 'Matthew & Son' etc., but when he put on his guitar and the band went off, the crowd got fed up after only one song and started to throw bits of paper and cigarette packets at him. They wanted the hits, fast songs with the band, and told him by their actions that they weren't happy. The band came back on and everything worked out alright in the end, and Cat Stevens was on top again.

The promoter of the Perth Town Hall at the time used to book four guys from up in Liverpool, advertise them as 'The Drifters' from the USA, and charge a fortune for the tickets. They used to pack the place out, as everyone loved The Drifters then with the great Ben E King on vocals and lots of number one records in their set list. The clever promoter couldn't go wrong, and he made loads of money, as nobody ever guessed. The only reason we knew is that we were in the next dressing room and could hear the scouse accents when they spoke (on stage they spoke/sang with American accents!)

The most embarrassing night, for me especially, was when we did support slot for Status Quo who had a number one smash hit with 'Pictures Of

Matchstick Men' at the time, and we played in a really nice venue, I think it was Glasgow Town Hall, with a massive stage and shiny floor etc. Status Quo had all their equipment at the back of the stage, and their drum kit was on a special drum rostrum, so we had to put our gear in front of theirs as we were on first. Everything was fine, we set up ready to go, and after 30 minutes we were on. We played about two songs and the vibration from the bass and the other guitars made the stage bounce, and with the bouncing my drum kit started to move on the shiny floor. I couldn't do anything about it, and panic set in as my cymbals went one way, the large tom-tom went another, and the bass drum slid to the front of the stage, and I was left with just a snare drum and a hi-hat. I could see Status Quo and all their crew doubled up laughing their heads off at the side of the stage, and the audience were laughing too. It had never happened to me before or since, and I was so embarrassed I wanted the ground to swallow me up so I could get out of there. From then on, I always made sure I had a carpet to put my drums on, that stopped them moving.

Looking back, it was a great life really. Even the boring travelling was brilliant when you saw some of the sights travelling through the highlands of bonnie Scotland: a really beautiful country, with breathtaking scenery and warm-hearted people to welcome us to each town we played in. We never made much money, but we enjoyed it.

This is the essential grounding you need as a growing musician: playing loads of gigs to different people every night, learning your craft as you go along. Making music is the most rewarding profession to be in, with creative people around you to inspire you to be the best that you can possibly be.

CHAPTER 3

The Cartoone Years

Cartoone was formed from The Chevlons in Glasgow,Scotland, 1967. The members were: Derek Greigan (Vocals/Bass), Mo Trowers (Rhythm Guitar/Vocals), Mike Allison (Lead Guitar/Vocals) and me, Charlie Coffils, on (Drums/Vocals). The band was managed initially by Gordon Allison (Mike's Dad). The Chevlons had toured Scotland for years, playing as far away as Carlisle, and were the first band to play the newly built ballroom in the Aviemore Ski-Centre. Derek was an original member of The Chevlons, but left to seek his fortune in London. In 1967, Derek phoned up Mike and asked him if we would be interested in coming down to London and forming a band together and writing some songs, with the view to obtaining a record deal.

The Chevlons played support to the following bands in and around Scotland:

The Hollies
The Searchers
The Beach Boys
The Tremeloes
Marmalade
Cat Stevens
The Merseybeats
The Drifters
The Move
Manfred Mann
The Kinks
Status Quo
and many more…

The band changed their name to Cartoone and we made our way to swinging London with about £40 between us (musicians never have money) in April 1967.

Derek Creigan met us all at Golders Green station (Derek lived with his wife and baby). Unfortunately for us, Derek couldn't put us up for the night, so we spent our very first night in London sleeping behind Golders Green station on wooden boxes.

After a sleepless and uncomfortable night, we walked across the road to the Wimpy Bar for breakfast, and very welcome it was too. Nothing like roughing it to make you appreciate the nice things in life (like a warm bed for instance).

A week had passed where we slept in various mates' flats/houses who lived in London and were decent enough to put us up for a couple of nights. Dean Ford, the singer in Marmalade, was very kind in letting us stay for a few nights in his flat.

Also we met another band who came down to London to seek fame and fortune, Mott the Hoople, who just happened to have a Transit Van and no money (figures).

Both bands got on really well together, with loads of Mickey taking and humour among everyone. Even though it was a difficult time for them moneywise, everyone was in high spirits and having the time of their lives in the 60s. London definitely was the place to be if you were a musician, so much happening, and so many bands were in London trying to make it in the music business. As history will tell us, Mott The Hoople had a massive hit called 'All the Young Dudes' in the early 70s. They were a great bunch of lads who knew how to have a good time, but still worked hard on their music, writing new songs every day.

We were getting fed up with being hungry and

skint all the time, so we all decided to get jobs. Mo worked on a building site, Mike worked in a shop, and I got a job with a firm who put ramps and wall safes etc. in hospitals. The guy who took me under his wing was called Nobby Clark, a lovely man, a real cockney who worked and played hard. He was always singing while he worked, and had a great sense of humour. Mo and I could afford a one room flat above a chip shop in a place called Belsize Park, and were able to eat properly once again, instead of living on bars of chocolate and biscuits.

After Derek and the rest of the band wrote two albums worth of songs, we contacted old friend Lulu, who gave us the phone number and address of the man who wrote her world famous number one song 'To Sir With Love' (USA/Billboard chart number one for eight weeks), the brilliant songwriter, Mark London. We phoned Mark first to arrange a time to come and see him.

When we got there, Mark greeted us in his dressing gown (he had just got out of the bath). Mark was over 6ft tall, a big man, around 15 stone, with a little goatee beard and a full head of black wavy hair. Originally from Canada, he was a larger than life personality with a great sense of humour.

So you can picture it: there was Mark sitting there in his dressing gown, listening to four guys from Glasgow singing their songs with great passion and excellent vocal harmony to him. Mark's reaction was immediate. He said that he loved the songs and wanted to get us in the studio right away.

The next day, Mark booked Cartoone into Regent Studios in Denmark Street, London and we recorded six songs with just two acoustic guitars and us four vocalists.

Mark then took that acetate to the USA to none other than the President of Atlantic Records, Ahmet Ertegun, and Jerry Wexler, his main partner and producer, who then worked out a deal with Mark for an advance of $65,000 (this is the figure I read in the papers but I don't know if it's true or not) to record the first album, and an option on the second album. Mark came back to London and we all signed the contracts at Heathrow Airport. Mark then flew back to the USA with the contracts and gave them to top music attorney, Steve H. Weiss, who looked after most of the big acts in the USA at the time. He then began all the legal stuff with Atlantic Records on Cartoone's behalf.

While Mark was away we got busy rehearsing

the songs to prepare for the recording session in a few weeks time. The band went to music arranger John Cameron's house. We sang all the songs and he recorded them onto a Reel-to-Reel tape so he could do the strings/horns/woodwind arrangements for a few of the songs that he thought needed it.

Mark decided he would bring in a friend of his, Peter Grant (manager of Led Zeppelin), and also Marion Massey (Lulu's manager) to form a co-management that would enable them to launch both the bands: Cartoone and Led Zeppelin. The idea was that Cartoone would support Led Zeppelin on their debut tour of the USA. The legendary, Harold Davidson, was brought on board as our PR Guru, so we had the best people looking after us.

Jimmy Page (formerly of The Yardbirds) was brought in as a guest guitarist to add some extra credibility to the project, and played his paisley pattern Fender Telecaster on the band songs, and his Gibson Acoustic on all the orchestral tracks on the album.

In retrospect, the initial idea was good because it would give new band, Cartoone, some exposure with their debut album (especially with Jimmy Page featured on the album).

The problems would come later when we were on a tour of the USA in support of Led Zeppelin, who were all fantastic outstanding individual musicians, and we obviously weren't in the same league as musicians in comparison. But that wasn't important, because in truth, Derek's very distinctive voice and our songs were really Cartoone. We supported him and helped him write and structure the songs when he only had a few lines written or half a song which needed a chorus etc. Derek preferred to be part of a band rather than a solo singer so he could bounce ideas off all of us, and we inspired him to create great music.

Although Derek is named as songwriter on most of the album, in truth, he could never have written them without the input of all of the rest of the band. We wrote all the songs together, as Derek had only bits of songs and ideas and we helped finish the songs, so it was always a Cartoone project writing all the songs. The album was made in DeLane Lea studios, London in 1968. It took three weeks to complete and we all thought at the time that it sounded fantastic (a typical 60s album, all violins/cellos and drums low in the mix, but with bags of echo on them and the vocals). The engineers were Dave Siddle, Brian Humphries and Eddie Kramer who later did most of the Led Zeppelin recordings. Mark London was the producer, and to listen to it now it sounds dated, but at the time it was a really well produced 60s album with great songs that grow on you the more you listen to them.

It was so exciting recording with the legendary Jimmy Page – sort of thing to tell your grandchildren about. As one of the most used session guitarists in the country, even before Led Zeppelin, I had read so much about him from music magazines in Glasgow. Jimmy had played on countless number one hits such as The Kinks' 'You Really Got Me' and Jet Harris & Tony Meehan's 'Diamonds' to mention just a couple.

We were all in awe when he came into the studio and we were introduced by Mark. Jimmy looked every inch the Rock Star with his slim build and long hair and handsome boyish face. He shook all our hands warmly and seemed friendly and down to earth with no ego at all.

You could cut the excitement with a knife as he took out his trusty paisley pattern Fender Telecaster (the same one he would later use on stage in the USA). It goes without saying we were all on a major high playing and recording with one of the best guitarists in the world.

I kept thinking as I looked over at him, 'Wow! That's Jimmy Page playing with us.' It was really surreal watching him play his guitar with a little unknown band like us.

We just did a quick run through of each song, and then went for a take. Jimmy was a 'OneTake' guitarist. Jimmy just became part of the band so effortlessly and fitted right in with us. He was so pleasant and easy to talk to as we listened to all the playbacks of the tracks we had just recorded. I congratulated him on his excellent guitar playing, particularly at the end of the track 'Let Me Reassure You', as he done this lovely country style guitar solo as the track faded out. Jimmy thanked me, and said that he really enjoyed playing with us, as he had been rehearsing with Led Zeppelin, and it was nice that he could help us out on our debut album.

I asked him about his new drummer, John Bonham, who Mark London had been raving about. Jimmy said that he was amazing, really loud, but with great feel and power on the kit. He said the band just gelled straight away, and after the first song they played at the rehearsals everyone was saying, 'F**k me. What a band!' especially their manager, Peter Grant, who was Mark London's best mate. Jimmy said that Led Zeppelin was a band made in heaven, and he couldn't wait to get onstage with them and do it live. We all hoped that both bands would do well, but Jimmy had no idea how massive Led Zeppelin would become at the time. He wished us all the best with the album.

Photo: Duffy© Duffy Archive (Front of Album Cover)

What a memory. I wish someone had taken a photo of us playing with Jimmy, it would have been priceless.

We spent 2 days with legendary 60s photographer 'Duffy' in his London studios in Holborn. He took loads of photos in the studios and in Hyde Park too. We had a great time; Duffy made us laugh with his banter and fantastic personality, he took the Mickey out of us being from Glasgow, and did a great Glasgow accent, which we all laughed at, as it was done in great humour. We loved being around Duffy, as he told some excellent funny stories about life and the celebrity world in general. You could tell Duffy knew his craft as he was so confident and assured. He directed us on what he wanted from us. I read later that David Bailey called him a cantankerous old b*****d, who loved to upset people just for an argument, but he was brilliant with us, and we loved being around him. Hopefully, he felt the same about us. I'm sure he did. Duffy didn't take any nonsense from anyone and did everything on his own terms. He was awesome and a pleasure to be around. One of those photos is proudly displayed on the front cover of our debut album, *Cartoone*, and four smaller photos were chosen for the back cover.

We will always be proud of that front cover of our first album. It looked so dark and moody, with a real atmospheric look about it which would definitely stand out in a record shop. Even by itself, without the Cartoone logo, the photo stands out as an iconic picture that will stand the test of time.

Lulu was also a frequent visitor to the studio to lend her support and encouragement. She was always so up and enthusiastic about our music and would often lend a hand with the backing vocals. Great voice and personality, she certainly helped create a great vibe, which is important when you have to make the 'magic' in the studio.

We used to go round her house in Compton Avenue in Highgate. It was a beautiful house, very tastefully furnished by Lulu. She had an amazing record collection in this gorgeous handmade large wooden coffee table, where I first discovered Harry Nilson. Lulu played me his album, which had that great song 'Without You'. I always got on really well with Lulu, as we had the same daft sense of humour. We had such a laugh hanging out with Lulu and Maurice Gibb her husband. I couldn't believe that she was younger than me, as she was already so rich, confident and self assured. I suppose that comes when you are so successful and have people falling over themselves to please you and cater to your every need. It must be amazing to be such a successful singer and have fame, with loads of money, and live in total luxury. I do envy her, but she is so talented and works so hard at her craft trying to be as perfect as possible. I think Lulu does deserve it all in my opinion.

Funny how only a handful of artists really make it big with riches etc., compared to all the great artists that I have heard and seen over the years who are trying to make it and will never be discovered or never have the chance to make it in the music business. It's so unfair, but that's life I suppose. I think you need someone with influence and connections to champion your cause and push you forward, but once you have the chance or the opportunity to shine in front of an audience, then you either have that certain 'magic' that will connect with them or you don't, and the audience will love or hate you. It really is that basic.

I felt really proud of us when I was walking in Piccadilly Circus in London after the album was released in the UK. In the front window of HMV they had a *Cartoone* display with photos and the album covers all on the window. It was a great feeling for me personally seeing our record with the Atlantic Records logo on. It made me so proud. This was just the release of the album. Imagine if it had sold big at number one. What would I have felt like then? Absolutely awesome.

Such a shame we didn't play any gigs in the UK to promote the album, as that would have helped the sales tremendously and maybe we would have built a fan base in the UK.

You need fans to phone up and badger DJs to play Cartoone songs and champion your cause. That's how you get records played and create a buzz about the band.

But sadly we never played any gigs in the UK with Derek as our lead singer.

Chapter 4

Happening For Lulu on BBC TV

The album was released in the UK first, and we had a front page on *New Musical Express* which was the big music paper along with *Melody Maker*. The band did a guest spot on the hugely successful *Happening For Lulu* show (28th December 1968) which was live on BBC1 every week, and it was a really good launch pad for Cartoone.

The show featured Lulu's husband at that time Maurice Gibb (BeeGees) and also The Tremeloes. Cartoone played their single 'Penny For The Sun' and Derek with Cartoone sang a duet with Lulu from their album called 'Toby Jugg'. The show went out live at prime time on a Saturday night around 6.30 p.m. What a buzz turning up at the BBC TV studios in White City, London.

The excitement we felt was electric, and it was surreal, as if we were dreaming it, but I definitely pinched myself, and yes it was true: we really were on TV that night playing live to the British public. We did the rehearsals in the afternoon. We sat in this room with Lulu and Laurie Holloway on piano, as she ran through some of the songs she would be singing that night. I didn't realise what a great singer Lulu was until I heard her that afternoon. It gave me goose bumps to hear her singing with such passion and control. Wow. Awesome singer.

Then we did a full rehearsal so the camera guys could get the angles for later. Then, an hour later, after lunch we did a full dress rehearsal of the entire show. Then an hour or so later we were live on BBC TV to the whole of the UK. Awesome and totally exciting.

Maurice Gibb had videotaped the show on his Video Recorder. He was one of the first people to have one in the UK. We all went back to his place in Kinnerton St, Belgravia to watch it and have a wee celebratory drink or two. Cartoone were now in the zone, with a front page photo of us on the *New Musical Express* (NME – 4th January 1969) thanks to Harold Davidson.

With a spot booked to appear on *Top Of The Pops* on 16th January, the world looked incredibly good for us. We kept thinking, 'any minute now we will wake up and it will all have been a dream'.

We recorded three songs live on BBC Radio and as I remember they turned out really good. Tony Blackburn was the top DJ of the moment and was playing our single 'Penny For The Sun' on his show. The single was selling reasonably well I think but was not a major seller. I remember listening to the radio in our little flat above the chip shop in Belsize Park with Mo, and they played the live stuff on the radio. It sounded so good, I wish we could have taped it then, but we didn't have a tape recorder. So frustrating.

The Beatles then released 'Hey Jude' which was an immediate massive number one hit for them. Everything the Beatles released at that time went straight to number one, and as Cartoone's single was in a similar tempo, 'Penny For The Sun' was overshadowed to say the least. Who can compete with The Beatles?

We weren't put off. In fact we felt absolutely excited. A new album released on the Atlantic Record label (one of the most famous and respected labels in the world), *Top Of The Pops* on 16th January 1969, a USA promotional tour in January 1969 to promote the new release of the *Cartoone* album, and a concert tour in support of Led Zeppelin from April to June 1969. Who wouldn't be excited? It's a dream come true for any band, never mind four musicians from Glasgow who, in their wildest dreams, would never have dreamt it, even with our vivid imaginations.

Just after the single 'Penny For The Sun' was released, I went along to visit my old workmate, Nobby Clarke, and as I walked into the little hut he based himself in, he was so pleased to see me again he nearly choked on his sandwich. Amazingly as we chatted about old times, 'Penny For The Sun' only came on the radio. I couldn't have planned it better. He loved the song so I gave him a signed copy of our album. He was so chuffed that he had worked with a 'Pop-Star' (ha ha!) and he would tell all his friends how he used to boss me around, and have me working my nuts off. A lovely old guy with a great personality: good old Nobby. God bless you mate.

CHAPTER 5

Top Of The Pops on BBC TV

What a great start to the year: 4th January1969, we were on the front page of NME, and had an appearance on *Top Of The Pops* (Thursday 16th January 1969). Here are some of the artists featured on the show:

Marmalade who had a number one with 'Obla-Di-Obla-Da' (Dean Ford – lead vocals).

Cartoone with 'Penny For The Sun' (Derek Creigan – lead vocals).

The Move with 'Goodbye Blackberry Way' (Carl Wayne – lead vocals).

Manfred Mann with 'My Name's Jack' (Mike D'Abo – lead vocals).

Long John Baldry with 'Mexico'.

My dad never validated me as his son (what his problem was, I'll never know) and was never affectionate or warm towards me. My sister, Linda, was always his favourite. He didn't have much time for my brother, John, and me. He was always quick to criticise me, and never praised me for anything. So I never knew what he thought of me, or if he even liked me, never mind loved me. Bit sad really, as I always tried my best to please him whenever he was around.

So imagine how surprised I was to hear from my mum that when they both watched me play drums with Cartoone on *Top Of The Pops*, my dad was kneeling in front of the TV and crying 'That's my son, my wee boy on TV'. Obviously he was finally proud of me at last.

Maurice Gibb (BeeGees) videotaped our performance on TOTP, and we all went back to Maurice's house in Kinnerton Street, Belgravia to watch it. Having seen the recording of 'Penny For The Sun', which the band had performed live in the studio (due to Musicians Union rules) and then mimed (to our own earlier recording) on the actual show. I thought that it was absolutely brilliant, much better than the album version, and I thought we all looked great on TV. I still don't know why it wasn't a hit after this excellent performance (wasn't meant to be I suppose), but at least I finally got to play a 'Silver Sparkle' Ludwig kit on TOPT.

All who watched the video that night, including Lulu and Maurice, agreed that Cartoone were brilliant on TOTP. Imagine how we felt: we had toured Scotland for years playing covers of songs by the BeeGees and other top twenty bands, and now here we all were, sitting in Maurice Gibb's house with Lulu, sipping champagne and celebrating, with Maurice himself going out of his way to tape our performance on the biggest music show in the UK for us, and now we had become quite close friends with both Lulu and Maurice. Life doesn't get better than that.

Maurice and I used to drive around in his posh cars: Rolls Royce, Bentley, you name it, he had it. He was a brilliant bloke to be around, as even though he was a pop star, he was so genuine and funny, you couldn't help but like him. We would sing along to songs that came on the car radio, even BeeGees songs, and we did harmony vocals together. Quite a good blend of voices we had as I remember.

Maurice was so kind and generous. He saw that

we didn't have any money and because both he and I were the same size and build, he gave me loads of his shirts and jackets. In all the promotional photos of Cartoone that were taken, I was wearing the clothes that Maurice gave to me. They fitted perfectly. My favourite was the blue silk shirt he gave me for my 21st birthday. It was a fantastic looking shirt that just made me look and feel like a million dollars. I have a photo of me wearing it in the recording studio. Even in black and white it looks great! (See the front cover photo of this book.) He also gave me two jackets; one was red suede and the other was brown leather, both the same style and cut.

Both Maurice and I had a bit of a problem with premature baldness. So we went to this 'Hair Clinic' in Green Street, London, and were pampered by these pretty young girls who used to rub this special cream into our hair, then sit us under an ultra-violet lamp and massage our heads (nice!). This was supposed to help our hair grow. It was so funny, as we sat there looking at ourselves and laughing. I said to Maurice, if only your fans could see you now. Maurice and I both lost most of our hair over the years in spite of that 'miracle' cream.

Maurice took me along to this tailor shop as I

needed a couple of suits for the USA promotional tour. Maurice had a wicked sense of humour, as he managed to talk me into getting this three piece pink herringbone suit, and convinced me that it looked absolutely fabulous, and said that nobody else would have a suit like that. I was so naive I believed him (nobody else would be daft enough to buy a suit like that). To think I actually wore that suit on American TV, unaware how awful it looked. I think that Maurice must have had many a laugh at the thought of me wearing that suit and me thinking that I was 'cool'. Somewhere in the archives of the many US TV stations we played on all over the USA they have the film of us wearing those awful suits – aarrgghh!

Maurice and I were always laughing and joking around, and for someone so young, he had done and seen so much already. He knew The Beatles as personal friends (how cool is that?) and John Lennon had given him his own Gibson black acoustic guitar as a present. Wow! Now just think how amazing that must be! We both grew up admiring and hero-worshipping The Beatles, and now Maurice was John and Ringo's mate. Ringo lived nearby so often came round to Lulu and Maurice's house for a drink and a singsong, with Dudley Moore playing piano, and they would party into the night (Lulu mentions this in great detail in her book *I Don't Want To Fight* by TimeWarner).

In my opinion, the BeeGees are easily one of the best singer/songwriting groups ever. Their catalogue of songs will live on forever. Even now at the time of writing this story the DJs are constantly playing BeeGees songs on the radio worldwide. My favourite two songs of theirs are 'Be Who You Are' and 'Immortality'.

*Mike Allison outside the Marriot Hotel
in Philadelphia on Promo Tour*

Mo Trowers enjoying himself on a break from Promo Tour

Derek enjoying a paddle in Chicago (USA-Tour '69)

Derek Creigan having some fun on the Promo Tour

PROGRAMMING CONSULTANT Bill Gavin, KYA program director Dick Starr and KYA personality Gary Schaffer are part of the antics of the Cartoone, a new English group on Atlantic Records. The occasion was a party honoring winners in San Francisco of the KYA and KOIT-FM "Cartoone" art contest promotion. Schaffer is at left, Gavin is in center with glasses, with Starr to the right of Gavin. The rest are members of the group.

That's me in front wearing my pink suit

Mike and friend in New York 1969

We visited one of Mike's uncles in New York (and his lovely dog)

61

CHAPTER 6

The USA Promotional Tour – January 1969

Mark London and Cartoone left for our USA promotional tour a couple of days after the TOTP show (Atlantic Records heard good reports from the show about our performance on it). It was Derek, Charlie, Mo, and Mike's very first time on a plane, never mind going to USA. Wow! We all felt so excited at the prospect of being on the American radio and TV shows etc.

When we landed on USA soil for the first time, the mood was spoilt a bit by me being strip searched by US Customs for who knows what they were looking for. They looked at all my personal belongings for about an hour, until they were satisfied that I wasn't carrying anything illegal. I must have obviously looked a bit suspicious with my long hair and dark glasses. Our spirits lifted when we saw the massive Limo with the driver waiting outside the airport to escort us to our hotel. For four poor guys from a tough city like Glasgow, coming to New York was like a dream come true.

As far as I can recall, the person who met us at the airport, and looked after us from Atlantic, was named Arthur: a really nice helpful guy I must say. He came to the Gorman hotel to pick us up and take us to Atlantic Records. We were looking forward to this. We had been listening to Otis/Booker T/ Solomon Burke/Aretha etc., etc., for years and now to come into this hallowed place... We kept thinking 'Is this real or what? I'm gonna wake up and it will all have been a fantastic dream.'

We were taken into the actual Atlantic Studio on Times Square, 1841 Broadway, New York, where all those great hits had been made. I couldn't resist the temptation to sit behind the drum kit that had been on all those records that I loved so much, even playing it dry without the microphones, it still sounded great to my ears. The Rascals had just finished recording a few hours ago, and you could still feel the vibe in the room. It was one of those magical and never to be forgotten moments in mine, and the band's, life.

We were given a list of new albums and told to

pick any records that we wished. Boy did we have a great time. Some of the records were only released in the USA and so were extra special. We all left Atlantic with a stack of records each,

(heaven for any music fan), including music from people like Otis Redding, Aretha Franklin, Ray Charles, Herbie Mann, Yusef Lateef and Bob Dylan to name just a few.

Before we left we were taken to meet Ahmet Ertegun and Jerry Wexler for the first time. I struck up a rapport with Ahmet straight away. He seemed to take a liking to me and made me personally feel at ease. We got on great, as he loved drummers as he thought they were the heart and soul of any band. He always said, 'If the band has a great drummer, then they are likely to be a great band.' I always agreed with him, as I think so too.

We appeared on various TV and radio stations in New York, Chicago, Houston, Detroit, Philadelphia, Minneapolis, Cleveland, Cincinnati, Pittsburgh, Boston, Montreal (Canada), San Francisco and Los Angeles, to name a few.

The whole trip ended with a VIP tour of the famous Walt Disney World and Marine-Land (Los Angeles), and going to see The Rascals in concert at the Anahiem Centre with the President of Atlantic Records, Ahmet Ertegun. Life doesn't get any better than that.

In New York, we were invited to see Led Zeppelin at their first gig in the USA at the Filmore East, as Zeppelin were the headline band that night, and Joe Cocker and his band opened up for them. We hadn't seen Zeppelin live yet, so we were excited to see them play. Peter Grant left our backstage passes at the stage door. We went backstage and said a quick hello to Page, Plant and Bonham. It was packed out, with the smell of marijuana filling the air. An announcement came over the speakers to tell everyone that John Paul Jones had been delayed, and that Jimmy Page would play some stuff to entertain us whilst we waited for JPJ to arrive.

Well I said I was impressed with Jimmy before in the recording studio, but this performance will stay in my memory forever. Jimmy sat there for half an hour and blew us all away with his amazing guitar playing. During this guitar virtuoso solo, there were many highlights, with everyone getting to their feet and applauding this brilliant guitarist, after he pulled off some awesome tasty, technically brilliant playing. At the end everyone was on their feet cheering. Then the rest of Led Zeppelin came on stage and blew us all away once more. What a band, so exciting to watch and listen too.

What a night of amazing music, I for one will never forget. The whole band just had that special something, and you just knew they were destined to be massive. I stood behind John Bonham and watched him perform on the drums. My jaw just dropped in amazement at some of the drumming he was doing. The guy was out of this world, a genius of drumming. That sort of talent is a gift from God, as it goes beyond the normal standard of great drumming. I knew then he was special and destined to be one of the great drummers of our time. Unfortunately, I didn't get a chance to talk to John that night other than to tell him what I thought of his drumming as he came off stage. What an exciting night, to be present at the birth of this great band was so extra special.

I hoped that when we came back to the USA to do our live tour supporting Led Zeppelin, we would get the same response from the American audience that they deservedly got. Wouldn't that be great!

CHAPTER 7

Conversation with a 60s PA

I spoke to the brilliant Elaine Harper who was Lulu's very first PA, and here is what she had to say:

I was employed as Lulu's first ever secretary/PA in the late 60s after the film 'To Sir With Love' was released, which she starred in with Sidney Poitier, and we both got on well from the start.

There were no computers, internet or mobile phones – I worked with an address book, a diary, typewriter and a basic telephone in a study at Lulu's London house. Luxury when travelling was a portable typewriter and, not possessing the 'work aids' around today, I depended on my own added skills of memory, common sense and plain dedication.

Contact outside working hours was the norm as arrangements, times and dates could change rapidly and, without mobile phones, the lack of instant contact, could at times, be very stressful. There was never a typical day – each one was different so I must admit boredom never set in.

I worked alongside Chris Cooke, Lulu's efficient and extremely capable Road Manager and Marion Massey, her very respected Personal Manager. Marion was one of the first female Managers in the music business and was highly regarded by all. She taught me so much in handling the work aspect and looking after a star of Lulu's calibre.

My role at a later date also became combined with the position of PA to Marion, which although adding to the workload gave me a great insight into the business side and made us all a tight-knit efficient unit that worked well, and when Lulu and Maurice Gibb were married my role expanded once again. Not excessively as Maurice, being one of the three Bee Gees, was looked after business-wise by Robert Stigwood, so it was mainly the personal side – an exciting time all round being associated with his talented brothers, Barry and Robin, too.

Travelling with Lulu took us to many parts of the world, sometimes on our own or with Chris and our own musicians. On the rare occasions Chris did not accompany us, I would check the sound levels and oversee the lighting plots at the venue. He instructed and taught me well, but we did not reckon with the situation that met me in Singapore.

The venue was at one of their large open air arenas and, as we had just flown in from New Zealand, there had been no time for a sound or lighting check beforehand. Not only did a huge monsoon occur at the start of the show cutting off all sound and lighting for a while, but when we were able to resume, I found myself in the Control Box with two Chinese men – one with limited English and the other with no English!

Going forth with that old cliché, 'The Show Must Go On', I do not think I have ever gesticulated, pointed, mouthed and mimed so much at one time in my life – Lulu and the band's performance received a fantastic reception and was a huge success – strangely enough so were the effects from the Control Box.

The 60s fashions were wonderful, innovative and fun with fantastic designers like Mary Quant, inventor of the mini skirt, Barbara Hulanicki, the founder of Biba, the brilliant textile designer, Zandra Rhodes, and the brilliant partnership of Celia Birtwell and Ossie Clark.

There were also fabulous hairdressers like Vidal Sassoon, the creator of the Mary Quant wedge Bob hairstyle, and Leonard, known for Twiggy's famous pixie cut. London's Carnaby Street and Kings Road were two of my regular haunts. It was a great time to experience the changes in fashion, but one night I did get it terribly wrong!

Lulu was appearing in Majorca. Maurice arrived to see the show and then he and Lu were flying off to another destination, so they were unable to attend *Georgie Best's party afterwards, but myself and the band attended as we were not flying out until the next day. I was wearing a new short, dark red, crochet dress, very trendy and chic, which had been specially made, but during the party it started to feel heavy and appear to get longer. There was just no explanation and it has remained a mystery ever since – it was not imagination or inebriation – maybe it had something to do with the wool and atmospheric conditions.* I left with a hem-line three inches longer than I had arrived with – *not many could say they started out wearing a mini dress and left with a midi.* Thank goodness the party had come to a close otherwise I may not have been able to drag myself away (literally).

Life in the 60s was exciting. The stars and celebrities that we worked with and knew were countless – a great many have gone on to become legends as have Lulu and the Bee Gees. Favourites of mine, to name a few from those days were the fabulous Carpenters who Lulu appeared with in Germany, Kenny Rogers who was then with The First Edition, Ray Stevens and Mama Cass, Glen Campbell, the hilarious Morecambe and Wise, and zany Spike Milligan, who actually taught me to eat with chopsticks at the famous *'Mr Chows Restaurant' in Knightsbridge, the American standup comedian/actor, Bob Newhart, Scott Walker, then a 1960s pop icon with the Walker Brothers, Peter Noone from Hermans Hermits, the lovely Cynthia Lennon,* popular *Georgie Fame, the very cool Tom Jones, fabulous Dusty Springfield, Les Harvey and Maggie Bell from Stone the Crows, the late great David Bowie, and of course, the very talented Cartoone.*

Cartoone were good friends of Lulu, Maurice and Marion, and when I first heard their 1969 album containing the haunting rendition of the track 'A Penny For The Sun', it became one of my long-time favourites. Maurice and Charlie had the same brand of humour so life was never dull when those two got together.

I have numerous recollections from the 60s – a great time to be around and I loved every minute of it!

Maurice, Lulu, Ken, Elaine and Marion Massey

Lulu and Elaine on tour

CHAPTER 8

The USA Live Tour (April–June 1969)

Cartoone returned to the UK to begin rehearsing for our first live tour of the USA where we would be onstage with some great bands such as Led Zeppelin, Santana, The Paul Butterfield Blues Band, Spirit, John Lee-Hooker, Arthur Brown's Crazy World and Vanilla Fudge to name a few.

A major problem occurred during rehearsals. We were told that Mike Allison had had a huge falling out with Derek and Mark London over the songwriting credits and other things. Mike decided that he didn't want to do the tour, and didn't agree with Derek taking all the credit for all the songs as it was a team effort, and thought that he and the rest of the band should get a credit too. Mike said that he wished to concentrate on his writing and recording and left the band, which didn't make sense to me, as we were just taking off in America, so why leave now? The irony is that years later in the future,

Mike's decision would turn out to be the best thing he ever did (more about that later in the story).

The band were in a bit of a panic, as we only had two months to record the second album and rehearse for what would be the biggest tour of our lives. This was to be presented to Atlantic Records President, Ahmet Ertegun, who would hopefully give us some more money to go ahead and record it properly (possibly in Atlantic Studios itself). The next problem was finding a guitarist at such short notice for the tour of the USA.

Mo and Derek suggested a really great guitarist they knew who was based in Glasgow, outlandish singer, Alex Harvey's brother, Les Harvey. Mark contacted Les by phone, and arranged to go and see him in Glasgow. As all accounts go, Mark was very impressed with Les's guitar playing, and by his girlfriend Maggie Bell, who had a fantastic powerful voice.

Mark was apparently so impressed that he brought Peter Grant (Led Zeppelin manager) to see the band play in Glasgow, obviously some sort of deal was made with Les and the new band (who were named by Peter Grant as Stone The Crows) because Les and Maggie came to London the next week.

Les began rehearsals with Cartoone for the tour.

We were rehearsing really hard to get ready for the USA tour. The only problem was that the songs on the first album had a full orchestra, and it was difficult to make them sound good with just lead guitar, rhythm guitar, bass guitar and drums. So the plan was to do a few of the songs that worked from the first album, and do all of the second album, which is mainly just the band with Les Harvey.

Les Harvey created a couple of his own songs to add to our set list. The set opened with me on drums and Les on guitar going hell for leather, playing this tune that Les had written, and after a few bars, the rest of the band joined in. It was a really up-tempo tune with Les making his guitar sound like a sitar by tuning it differently then, as I carried on the beat during the number, Les then tuned his guitar back to normal tuning before the rest of the band joined in. It was a really exciting fast number that built nicely. Good start to the set, and it got the band, and hopefully the audience, in the mood.

We had done our best in the time given to prepare ourselves for whatever was ahead on the USA tour. On the last day of rehearsals, Maggie Bell came along to have a listen, and she ended up jamming with us on a few old blues songs. It sounded really good, and Maggie sure had a powerful voice and knew how to sing the song with passion.

We gave Mick Ralphs (Mott The Hoople) the key to our Gloucester Road flat in London, so he could look after it for us while we were on tour. As most of them hadn't a place to stay, I believe the whole band moved into the flat (as we found out on our return to the UK).

Before we left for the USA, Stone The Crows went into Pye Studios, London using all Cartoone's equipment, including my drum kit. Mark and Peter wanted to do a demo of the band to let Ahmet and Jerry hear how they sounded.

Obviously Mark and Peter were hoping to get a deal with Atlantic Records for Stone The Crows, and felt confident the demo would make that happen for them.

We were really on a high in anticipation of the tour as the Limo came to take us to the airport. Dennis Sheehan, our tour manager, had everything organised for us, as he had already been briefed by Mark London. No problems with US Customs this time around; the band and especially me swept straight through without a hitch. Arthur from Atlantic Records was there to meet us again. Everyone, including Arthur, was very excited at the thought of Cartoone playing their first live gig in the USA at the world famous

Madison Square Gardens in New York. Wow!

We all arrived at the Gorman Hotel and put our luggage in the rooms before going to the venue. Coming down in the elevator was Jeff Beck and Rod Stewart, who introduced themselves and said they were playing the Filmore East the next night. We told them we would come to see them if time permitted. Jeff said he would leave some tickets for us at the door and wished us luck for tonight.

We were so excited when we arrived at Madison Square Gardens for the sound check. The place was really awesome inside, with one of those stages that turns around, with a band on either side. Dennis took us all backstage to see our equipment. Derek, Mo, and Les had been sponsored by 'Rickenbacker' who gave them guitars and amplifiers for the tour. Led Zeppelin had the same, and I believe Jimmy hated the Rickenbacker Amps. He much preferred his Marshall 200 watt stack he used normally back in the UK.

I got a deal along with John Bonham to have the

same kit from Ludwig Drum Company. John's kit was maple wood and mine was canary yellow, I don't know why I didn't ask for Silver Sparkle as I had always wanted that kit, but I chose Canary Yellow. The two kits looked wonderful set up together. They were both the same sizes too:

Snare: 6.5in x 14in
Bass drum: 26in x 18in
Small tom-tom: 14in x 16in
Large tom-tom: 18in x 18in

Powerful kit or what? And the best thing was, because both kits were custom handmade, they were so light you could lift the bass drum with two fingers. Beautiful workmanship by Ludwig. John had been playing his kit for a while now and was used to it. My kit back in the UK was a Ludwig super-classic of standard sizes so this was a big kit in comparison. John was kind enough to show me the best way to set the kit up and how to sit at it for maximum effect, which was completely the opposite of how I normally sat: very high, looking down on the drums. This style used by Bonham, was to sit very low and have the drums surrounding you and leaning towards you, as you basically looked up at them, as it's impossible to sit above a 26in bass drum, unless you're a giant.

I was so impressed by John Bonham, both as a person, and as a fantastic drummer. He was such a kind and helpful guy. This was in the early days, when Zeppelin were breaking into the USA, and the buzz was all around about them. He came over as an ordinary friendly down to earth guy, who was an incredibly talented genius drummer.

I discovered that we had the same tastes in music, which surprised me, as he loved all the soul and Tamla stuff, plus the Godfather of soul himself, James Brown. After seeing him play before at Filmore East and other gigs on our promo tour, I thought he was an out and out rocker, but he loved all sorts of music. I had never seen anyone play drums that loud or that fast – amazing technique and drive. John Bonham was ahead of his time, so inventive and clever.

His drum solo using his hands was something you had to see to believe. Awesome. He would play so loud with his hands and feet, and when he picked up the sticks to carry on the solo, John took it to another level. Words can't express how good a drummer this guy was. You had to be there watching him play to experience the magic that was

John Bonham. Definitely the best drummer of his time if not of all time. I remember watching from the side of the stage with Carmine Appice who was the drummer with Vanilla Fudge. Zeppelin were playing 'How Many More Times' and we both turned to each other and said, 'F**k Me' as we marvelled at how John's technique and inventiveness blew us away during his set.

Although John was amused that Karen Carpenter of The Carpenters was voted best drummer over him in a pop magazine poll. You must be joking. Karen had a wonderful singing voice, but couldn't come close to attaining the level of technique and groove that Bonham had achieved. She was a great singer, yes, but not on the same level as a drummer, in my opinion.

I knew that John Bonham was a far superior drummer to me, but I was of the attitude that I also had my own style of playing. Maybe it wasn't as impressive or awesome as John, but I felt that what I may lack in technique, I more than made up for in feel for the music, and laying down a good groove within the band can be just as important. He inspired me and made me strive to be a better drummer than I was.

CHAPTER 9

The Moment of Truth for Cartoone

It was Cartoone's turn to do a sound check and also our first try out of our new gear. Dennis Sheehan got everything ready for us. Les started proceedings by playing his new tune. I joined him on my beautiful new drum kit (even the smell was gorgeous) and we were off into the groove. It sounded really good, but Derek's voice was a bit hoarse (air-con in our hotel rooms made it very dry). The PA System was absolutely awesome with all the band going through it, including the drums. You could hear everything. It was really amazing. We cut the sound check short to try and save Derek's voice for the show in the evening. Mark arranged for Dennis to take Derek to see a throat doctor that afternoon to look at his throat and give him some medication to help ease the soreness.

Showtime, and Derek was feeling a lot better now. We were feeling so excited at the thought of being on stage at Madison Square Gardens where we had all watched world championship boxing matches such as Muhammed Ali vs. Joe Frazier on TV back in the UK. Someone came and knocked on the dressing room door: 'Five minutes to curtain guys.' Then the nerves kicked in. All the self doubt came flooding back. Had we rehearsed enough? Should we have toured Europe first, just to get our confidence up with playing live? Should we have hired an orchestra and done the songs properly? The answer was yes to all those things, but it was too late now. We were on in five minutes, and there were only us four lads. 'So here goes nothing!'

The announcement was made:

'Ladies and Gentlemen. The new sound from the UK. Please welcome Cartoooooone!'

I rushed out first and laid down the beat on my beautiful drum kit for the start of the set. Les came out next and started his tune. Mo and Derek were next, then we got under way, and I must say, it sounded really good. We ended the song with a blistering solo from Les Harvey and the audience cheered. What a relief – a good start for the evening.

We began to play 'Knick Knack Man' with Les and Mo playing nice guitar in unison, then Derek started to sing, or should I say croak. His voice sounded awful, all throaty, breaking up. Poor Derek. What a night for this to happen with all of New York's finest media reporters there to see the show. I dreaded to think what they would write about the band.

Derek's voice got worse as the set went on, so Les quickly said that we would do longer solo's with the drums and guitars to give Derek's voice a break. Mark London just walked away shaking his head. To be honest, we couldn't wait for the set to end. It was torture for Derek trying to sing. Finally, we finished the set to polite clapping and rushed off stage back to the dressing room. Maybe next time it would be better.

The next morning we woke up to the news that Cartoone had 'bombed' at the Gardens, and things didn't look good for Cartoone with Atlantic Records President, Ahmet Ertegun, due to make a decision on the second Cartoone album *Reflections*. We had an appointment to see Ahmet later that morning (this was meant to be a celebration meeting after a triumphant gig, but after last night, who knew?)

Mark London looked really worried as he entered Ahmet Ertegun's office. We sat in another office waiting. No one knew what would be happening next. I supposed it would be up to fate to decide the future of Cartoone. We all sat there in silence, except for Les, who was only standing in for us anyway, so it wasn't his problem as he had his own band, Stone The Crows, to consider when he got back to the UK.

CHAPTER 10

What A Difference A Day Makes

Mark came out of the office looking very sombre. He said that he had 'something to tell us'.

He came straight to the point: 'Atlantic Records are not going to release the second album, and they have decided, after last night's poor show and the mediocre sales of the first album (85,000 copies), that they would take up the option in the contract to drop the band from their roster of acts.'

Whoa! What a f*****g shock! Major! Wow!

We didn't know what to do or say. We felt numb at being rejected by Atlantic and couldn't believe that the second album wasn't going to be released. What a devastating thing to happen to the band, after only one gig. Okay it was a very important gig in front of the US Media, but this was a bit drastic. Unfair! Surely Atlantic would think again about this and give us another chance? Mark said Cartoone had had their one chance and blew it. The decision was made – no going back.

Mark said that the band could carry on with the tour, as it was all arranged and planned for anyway. We didn't know what else to do. Our manager, Mark London, had lost faith in us and said he wasn't interested in managing the band anymore now that Atlantic had dropped us. What a difference a day makes! Before the concert at Madison Square Gardens, Cartoone could do no wrong, and now the day after we get all this bad news. It was very hard to take in, as all the hype around the band was huge. So much was expected of us and, to be fair, we did begin to believe all the hype ourselves.

So there we were, four guys from Glasgow, Scotland, far away in America, way out of our depth with no one to turn to for help or advice on what to do next. We were in complete shock. We never expected anything like this to happen, as everything was going great.

Looking back, maybe Ahmet never listened to the second album due to our performance at MSG. Maybe Mark played him Stone The Crows' demo instead, and that might have put the final nail in Cartoone's coffin. We found out later that Ahmet signed Stone The Crows, with Mark London as their producer and Peter Grant as co-manager. So my theory does make sense considering the circumstances at the time. Suddenly, Cartoone didn't look such a great prospect after the MSG gig, and Stone The Crows, with the powerful voice of Maggie Bell and Les Harvey on guitar, with a much heavier sound might appeal to the new changing tastes of America.

Led Zeppelin were already climbing up the US charts, so it seemed that America had fallen out of love with the softer melodic sound of Cartoone and wanted the new heavier sound of Zeppelin, with heavy riffs and long guitar solos.

I suppose it's the usual story. We as the band rely on our manager for everything, but when the manager splits and puts his energy into another band, we are left high and dry with nowhere to go. That's Rock-N-Roll and the music business folks – it stinks!

Mark London flew back the next day to the UK, and we prepared to carry on with the rest of the tour. Hopefully, this would be the best therapy for us and we could try and make something good out of a bad situation. Suddenly, the limo and driver were gone and the small little entourage that Atlantic had assigned to look after us was quickly taken away. Cartoone were now treated like yesterday's news, discarded to the land of the 'Unwanted Bands/ Artists' where so many have gone before.

This is the other side to the Rock-N-Roll story: the tough, shape up or ship out attitude in 1969 of the major league record companies then, and probably even more so now. The sad fact is that if the album had sold millions worldwide, it wouldn't have mattered how bad or good Cartoone were live because, as everyone knows, money talks. And why should Atlantic drop a million selling band? They may be ruthless, but they're not stupid. No matter how much the media tried to bring the band down, and say they 'bombed' at The Gardens, no one would have given a damn as long as the records sold. Atlantic would have been all over Cartoone, telling us not to be down-hearted, and probably bringing in the orchestra and session singers to give Derek a bit of support and confidence, hiring the best doctors money could buy to look after Derek's throat.

The second album would have been re-recorded, no expense spared, with Jimmy Page hired to add more flavour to the sound and Atlantic Studios put at the band's disposal. Atlantic and Mark London would have been counting their millions and telling the band how great they were, and that The Gardens was just a little blip in the Cartoone road to success. If only this was the case, but as history or fate tells us, the album only sold 85,000 copies, and that's nowhere near a million in anybody's calculations.

Let's get back to reality. We were basically finished if things didn't pick up on the tour so we could start selling some albums. By the time we played the next gig, Derek's throat was much better, and Les Harvey was absolutely sensational. He really inspired the band. I was especially inspired by Les's playing. He brought the best out of me as I would play off Les and vice versa.

By the third gig, we were starting to sound like a band once more, enjoying playing tight again. Derek, Mo and myself were even doing three part harmony in 'Knick-Knack-Man' and other songs. This helped fill out the sound of the band. 'Come and Sit By Me' was becoming a good live crowd-pleasing song which went down well, especially with Les's guitar playing and soloing.

As we all realised this was the last tour we would ever play together, we began to enjoy the moment of being on stage in the USA in support of the best group ever: Led Zeppelin. Zeppelin exploded onto the scene over in the USA. Everyone went crazy over them and the buzz moved faster than anything as word got out that this phenomenal band were coming. How could any band compete with that, never mind poor old Cartoone, who's music was the opposite of what Zeppelin were doing, more Buffalo Springfield, or Harry Nilson, The BeeGees, than Led Zeppelin.

Looking back, supporting all these great bands was a good idea from an exposure point of view, but the audience were made up of heavy rock Led Zeppelin fans, due to the Zeppelin debut album being number one in the US charts at the time. The fans weren't really interested in Cartoone and our style of pop-music. They wanted heavy riffs, thundering drums, and rock god Robert Plant singing.

The most intimidating gig that we had to play was The Grande Ballroom in Detroit. I had a chance to practice with John Bonham, as he helped me set up my kit once again. Both kits looked great together, being the same size with massive bass drums (26in), mine Canary Yellow, and his Maple Wood. As I said before, John was the nicest guy you could meet, so natural and friendly with no obvious big ego at the time. As I watched him playing, I must admit I did try and copy some of his less hard drum licks, but he was such an amazing drummer with a great natural technique, that it was virtually impossible. But at least I can say that I practiced with John Bonham. Not many drummers can say that.

All through the tour, the Zeppelin guys were brilliant and really friendly with us, especially Jimmy Page and John Bonham. They treated us great and always had time for us to have a chat and talk about everything from guitars, drums, bands, the blues, and great songs and artists we all loved. They all were obviously told by Peter Grant that Atlantic had dropped us, but they never mentioned it or let on that they knew.

It was very hard for us to watch Zeppelin's star soaring, with more and more people coming to see them at the gigs, and us trying to stay positive and enjoy the moment onstage, and trying not to think of what was ahead.

We were never allowed into Zeppelin's inner circle (Circle Of Trust) and they always kept us at arm's length and just spoke to us at the gigs. They were always very friendly but we never hung out together or went to clubs with them.

So sorry you fans out there who were looking for new revelations of Rock-N-Roll mayhem with the Zeppelin guys. It never happened as we were not part of their inner circle I'm afraid.

One night, the opening band didn't turn up so it meant that Zeppelin and Cartoone had to play two sets each. We opened the evening playing our set as best we could and received reasonable applause from the mainly Zeppelin crowd. With everyone being impressed with Les Harvey's guitar playing and soloing (even Jimmy Page). Zeppelin came on after us and played their first set, an incredible exciting hour set, with Jimmy Page pulling out some great solos (with and without the 'Violin Bow'), and John Bonham amazed everyone with his power and technique in his drum solo 'Pat's Delight' soon to become 'Moby Dick' on the second album.

We then had to go back on after Led Zeppelin. Jeez – how do you follow them? How could I even think of going on and playing the drums after everyone had witnessed John Bonham in full flight? Anyway myself and the band just thought 'F**k It! There is no way we can upstage Zeppelin,' and so we just gave it our best shot and played our asses off, with Les playing his best ever. The crowd reacted really well surprisingly and gave us and Les a warm reception. I did notice that Jimmy Page and the rest of the band were watching from the side of the stage perhaps hoping to pick-up some tips (joke!). We just started to gel that night, and finished off the set with an old 'Sam & Dave' song called 'Hold On I'm Coming'. It lasted 20 minutes and we funked it up. The audience were on their feet dancing and John Bonham was laughing and enjoying it in the wings. He loved all the soul stuff. It was our best night so far, and we felt as if we had given Zeppelin a run for their money for a change (ha ha).

Another memory I have is in Chicago, when Les Harvey and I went to the Chicago Museum. Les was trying to bring some culture into my life, and we spent about an hour playing this amazing tubular drum sounding sculpture. It featured loads of tubes hanging down from the ceiling of different thickness, and you hit them with these special mallets, and the sound was fantastic. I wonder if it's still there?

One of the best gigs that Cartoone played was in Chicago. Spirit were the headline band and Cartoone had the slot before them. Opening the show was the legendary John Lee Hooker who just sat on a chair and played a sensational set of down-home blues all by himself. Awesome. He was the real deal, a proper bluesman.

To think that as 'The Chevlons' we had covered John's songs in our set touring Scotland and here he was supporting us in concert. There is no justice in this life. John should have been the headline act as his music started us all off in the beginning. It seems to be all about selling records, and John was a cult figure rather than a top ten act, so that's how they treated their own legends back then in the USA.

Anyway, John really put us in the mood for playing after listening to him. Cartoone took to the stage with new found confidence. Something just happened that night, call it magic if you like, but we were hot and played the best we have ever played. In the middle of the set, Les took his usual solo but this time the band followed his lead by joining him at different points in the solo, encouraging him to play even better.

Les played with feedback, wah-wah pedal, playing some amazing stuff, then he tuned the guitar so it sounded like a sitar. He was outstanding, and the whole audience were on their feet cheering us (our first standing ovation). We could do no wrong that night – it was brilliant. Everything we did gelled, and the things we tried just seemed to work unrehearsed. We were just spontaneous with the music and let it take us with it to the final few bars of the song/tune. Definitely our best gig yet without a doubt.

I finished off the night with me and Dennis going to a club with John Lee Hooker. When we got in there it was absolutely packed with a great band of musicians onstage and an amazing atmosphere. John asked me if I would like to go onstage and have a jam with him and the band. Of course I said yes. I got to share the stage with John Lee Hooker. We played 'Dimples' and a guy called Luther sang this fantastic song called 'Sweet Home Chicago' that grooved like nothing I have ever experienced. The hairs on the back of my neck were standing up and a glow went up and down my spine.

This was better than any drug, to play music this good with such feeling, all playing as one. This was the real deal: genuine down home proper blues played by experienced authentic bluesmen. Inspired by this awesome band, I played the best drums I have ever played, and I think everyone enjoyed it as they were all chanting and cheering at the end.

It was the most exciting music I have ever played in my life. As the first few bars of each song began, I kept it simple and tried to be cool and just play drums. I just floated within the music. It was truly unforgettable, and to share that experience with my mate Dennis Sheehan was awesome. Dennis told me afterwards that I was fantastic – a magical night of music.

The final gig that Cartoone played together was in Boston. It was very much a mixed emotional night, as we all played our hearts out and really tried to enjoy the gig, but we all knew this was the last time we would ever play together onstage. Les Harvey was his usual brilliant self, playing one awesome solo after another, and Derek sang his heart out and sounded great. But sadly no one from the media was listening anymore.

There was a fantastic photo of us onstage in our last performance and Dennis Sheehan had it. I have never seen it since, it's probably lost. Just like the original 'Master Tapes' of the second album 'Reflections' – lost and never to be found again.

Front Page of NME with Cartoone – 4ᵗʰ January 1969

Chuck and Derek in Chicago on USA tour '69

Me and Derek on tour in the USA

Derek at London Airport in 1969

CHAPTER 11

Isn't Life Crap Sometimes

We returned to England with no money, depressed at being dropped and losing our manager at the same time. We all just went our separate ways. The band felt numb and unable to pick ourselves up from the black hole that loomed before us. Rejection is a serious business at that level, especially as the band had so much exposure from the TV and music papers. Even we began to believe the publicity that was written about us. All the hype surrounding the band at the time and the high expectations from us made it much harder for us to go to any other record company for another deal. Word travels fast in the music business.

I remember years later the same type of thing happened to another UK band called Brinsley Swhwarz, which featured the excellent Nick Lowe as the main singer/songwriter. They invited all the music press and flew them over from the UK to a special gig in New York, all expenses paid etc., only for the same music press to absolutely destroy them in print in their various music papers. How ungrateful and spiteful is that?

But having what they called 'bombed' at Madison Square Gardens, and having had a taste of some minor success over in USA, we were all really demoralised and had lost all confidence to carry on. If only we had toured the album live around Europe first, and then we would have known what worked and what didn't. But coming from weeks in a rehearsal room in a pub in Chiswick, London to Madison Square Gardens is a lot to ask of any band. I suppose some would say that being flung straight in at the deep end any band would find out if they were ready or not for the big stage and all the trappings. The fact that we bombed shows that we definitely weren't ready to play MSG or any other big concert hall at the time.

I was so devastated at how quickly the rug can be pulled from under you without really a valid reason that I could see, other than our first gig, was crap. So what?

We had signed a contract with Atlantic Records, but the contract was always in the record company's favour, as they dropped us like a stone. I couldn't understand why before we played Madison Square Gardens, everything was so good, and the record company believed in their product.

A quote in a music magazine from Jerry Wexler said that 'in 1969 the two UK bands we have the most faith in long term are Led Zeppelin and Scottish band Cartoone.'

Atlantic couldn't do enough for us. Nothing was too much trouble and no expense was spared to keep us happy. We were just so innocent and naive to think that the record company would still give us another chance after letting them down by playing a crap gig at Madison Square Gardens in front of the world media.

On the tour, Les had been really impressed with my drumming. He said I was brilliant and had improved so much since he first played with me in rehearsals a few months ago. Probably it was touring with all the different bands, and playing every night, plus being inspired by watching and practicing with John Bonham. A lot of his magic had rubbed off on me. He was going to talk to Mark and Peter to see if I could be the new Stone The Crows drummer.

Little did Les and I know at the time of us touring

the USA, Mark and Peter had already chosen and hired a new drummer for Stone The Crows. It was ex John Mayall drummer Colin Allen.

After thinking things through, I decided that I would always love music, but the music business stinks, and I just wanted out of it. There is no loyalty or fair play. Musicians are just stuffed by the managers and record companies and left to sink or swim. I sold my beloved Ludwig drum kit for £150 and walked away from the music business and all its bullshit.

Four weeks after staying in the luxury five star Beverley Hills Hotel in Los Angeles I was back in England, broke without a penny to my name. I realised that I had to get a job, and went to the Job Centre to register with them.

The guy who interviewed me and took down all of my details, said that he was also a drummer in his spare time, and to top it all, he had only purchased my beloved Ludwig Drum Kit from the shop I sold it to the week before he met me. He knew this because the skin on the beater side of the bass drum still had the Cartoone logo that Mike Allison had painted on it. What a crazy world we live in, the chances of that happening and me meeting him must be a million to one.

I didn't know whether to laugh or cry, so I just wished him luck with the kit and left to apply for my first job weeks after coming back from the USA tour.

The one thing I am thankful for is nobody can take away the memories of those two great years where we were discovered by Lulu, Mark London, Marion Massey and Peter Grant. We went on to tour with all those fantastic world class bands like Led Zeppelin, were signed to one of the most respected record companies in the world, Atlantic Records, had the opportunity to be close friends with Lulu and Maurice Gibb who was a really genuine nice person who loved life, and we really became good buddies. It's a shame I lost contact with them after Cartoone split. We appeared on top TV shows in UK like *Top Of The Pops* and *Happening For Lulu*, a TV show in Berlin, Germany with a DJ and a little dog. We did TV and radio shows all over the USA.

I could have contacted Lulu and Maurice to ask for their help, as I was totally broke, but call it pride or whatever, I never saw either of them again after that, and I wanted them to remember me as a genuine friend and not someone who was just after them to scrounge money from them. So I left it like that, and took the decision never to contact them again.

And so ends the Cartoone Story, with a lot of 'if only' and, if I'm honest, a lot of bitterness at the time on my part, as I got a taste of the big time and had the rug pulled from under me. It was like being given a million pounds and we were allowed to have it our bank account and see it on our statements, but then we were told to give it all back leaving us with nothing: no money, no propects, and nobody would touch us with a barge pole due to the stigma of being dropped by Atlantic Records. In bitterness and frustration I smashed the album over my knee and put Cartoone behind me. I never saw or played it again for another 30 years, when I bought it in an old record store by chance. I was very depressed at the time and developed a stammer which was very frustrating. I was never the same person after that experience. I had lost all faith in life, and to be truthful, to this present day, I have never really gotten over the rejection by Atlantic Records. I was never the same drummer ever again.

So remember all you budding rock stars out there. If you have talent, get out of your bedroom and play some gigs, make sure you can do it live, and don't believe the hype. But most of all don't be put into the same position as us, going straight from rehearsal studio to an MSG live gig. That was dumb, but it seemed a good idea at the time. When you're young, you think you're invincible and have no fear of failure.

Led Zeppelin played a secret gig in Sweden first to see if it worked live in front of an audience and to get the reaction to the band. It was also for the band to hear how they sounded onstage and give them the confidence in themselves and the band before going to the big gigs in the USA. We should have done the exact same, then we would have sorted the problem before we reached the USA and Madison Square Gardens and not ended up embarrassing ourselves.

There I was on tour in the USA and staying in the luxury Beverley Hills Hotel with the sun shining and walking down Sunset Strip in LA. Then four weeks later, I'm sitting in Dennis Sheehan's spare room with just a suitcase, my drums, a mattress on the bare floorboards, and nothing else. I had £20 in my bank and a few dollars that I had from the USA. It was soul destroying, and very hard to take in.

But I will forever be grateful to Dennis Sheehan,

our excellent tour manager. Dennis and his wife Lisa rented out their spare room to me and gave me the run of the house. I think I would have definitely crashed and burned from bitterness and depression if it wasn't for Dennis and Lisa. They were both good true friends who cared about me and got me through a really tough time. I had never felt so alone in my life, and they were there for me.

It was very painfully difficult seeing Stone The Crows take off with Mark London and Peter Grant as their manager, and Dennis Sheehan as their new tour manager, after I was left high and dry with no money or prospects. Life can be so cruel sometimes, but, hey, you have to get on with it. You can't allow yourself to lay down and die. I had my chance and it didn't work out. No use feeling sorry for myself. I have to accept what happened and learn to live with the good memories and try to forget the bad. Life is what you make it and I intend to be positive and have a good life, to relish and enjoy the good times and endure the bad times.

After Stone The Crows' second album, *Teenage Licks*, came out, Dennis invited me to come along to their gig at the Marquee in Wardour Street, London. I met Les and Maggie for the first time since the

USA tour, and we went to the pub next door. Maggie and Les were very kind and complimentary to me, especially about my drumming. Little did they know I had sold my drums and given up the music business. I introduced my wife Jackie to them, and we then went to their gig and they were absolutely sensational. Maggie and Les were fantastic and the rest of the band were superb, with the excellent Colin Allen on Drums. I never ever saw Les or Maggie after that gig. Dennis was away a lot tour managing Stone-The-Crows, and his wife, Lisa, was also away periodically with her successful career as a model. So basically I had the whole house to myself, which to be truthful was very lonely, and I didn't enjoy it much.

After a couple of months I got a surprise phone call from my mum. She said that John wasn't getting on with my dad and asked me if she could send him to London to be with me. Dennis wasn't around, so I asked Lisa if my brother John could come and stay until I could sort something out. Lisa very kindly said yes and I phoned my mum the next day to tell her.

Jeez, as if things weren't tough enough with my life, I would now have the added responsibility of my 13-year-old brother!

A week later, I was standing on the platform in Kings Cross Station waiting to greet my little brother. It had been over a couple of years since I saw him last, and I was curious to see how much he had grown. John came off the train looking thin and very tired. I gave him a huge hug and told him not to worry as everything would be alright now. He was very quiet, and it took a while to get him to relax and open up about what had been happening at home. We got back to Lisa and Dennis's place, and Lisa prepared a meal for us both as she could see that John was tired and a bit in awe of being in London. She made us feel welcome and tried to put John at his ease.

John and I stayed with Dennis and Lisa for another eight months before we found a place to stay in Ealing. A couple of months later, my mum left my dad and brought my sister, Linda, to London. She did to my dad what he had done to her so many times over the years; she left him without a word of warning. I managed to find them a flat, living with another mother and daughter in Ealing, so things started to look up for John now my mum and sister, Linda, were around to keep him company.

In late 1970 I had met my future wife Jackie, and saw John, mum and Linda less and less. Jackie and I became really close over the next year, and we were married in 1971. So I'm sorry to say John was now my mum's responsibility once again, as I had a new wife to look after and build a life with.

I always felt guilty about leaving John and putting him back with our mum and sister, as we had become very close over the 2 years he lived with me. We did loads together, and I showed him London and tried my best to be an example to him and grew to love him as a brother again.

I think he took it very hard and missed me a lot, but he had to make his own life in London, and have a career to give him some sort of future.

Derek in
the
studio,
laying a
vocal
track for
the 2nd
album

Derek in Boston on USA tour 1969

Chuck and Mo outside their London Flat

Leslie and Mo having a jam on USA tour in Detroit hotel 1969

L-R:Leslie Harvey, Mo Trowers, Derek Creigan (pipe) in New York,USA tour 1969.

Mo and Derek outside their London flat in 1969

Me on drums (before the cancer started)

CHAPTER 12

After Cartoone
– The Second Beginning

I had turned my back on the music business and hadn't played drums for so many years when, on the 18th July 2000, I got a phone call from my brother-in-law, Winston, who used to be a member of The Aces and played guitar on the number one record with Desmond Decker & The Aces, 'The Israelites', back in 1968. He lives in the beautiful island of Majorca with his family. A friend of his, Neil, was having his 50th birthday party in Majorca, and wanted to have a band play at his villa. Winston was asked to form a band especially for this function which the whole village of S'Arraco near Andraxt was invited to, even the mayor and his wife.

Chris, my other brother-in-law, and I flew out on the Friday morning, the 21st July 2000, and arrived in the afternoon at about 3 p.m. and booked into the hotel. After we freshened up and put on our t-shirts and shorts (bloody hot – 85 degrees in the shade), we made our way to the rehearsal rooms to meet the rest of the band. I was shocked and excited when I met the rest of the band, as the sax player was none other than one of my great all-time favourite sax players Molly Duncan, ex Average White Band member, who now lived in Majorca. The rest of the band were as follows:

Chantelle Baker (USA) – Lead vocals
(backing singer to Gloria Estefan/Chaka Khan)

Molly Duncan – Sax
(formerly Average White Band)

Daniel Roth (USA) – Keyboards
(various bands from Van Morrison etc.)

Winston Robins – Guitar/vocals
(formerly Desmond Decker & the Aces)

Chris Robins – Bass guitar
(London session player)

Charlie Coffils – Drums/vocals
(Formerly Cartoone)

Jose Carlos – Harmonicas

The gig took place in a beautiful village set in a valley half an hour's drive from Palma. An open air gig on a big stage, the air was cool as it was now

8.30 p.m. We did a sound check, and it was good. We then went to have something to eat and chill out until the performance. We called ourselves The Old Farts for a laugh, as we were all over the age of forty, except for Chantelle.

At 10 p.m. we did our first set. What a band – it just grooved from the first bars. I was in musical heaven and I didn't want it to end. From 'Black Magic Woman' to 'Unchain My Heart' and James Brown's 'I Feel Good', the set just flew by. I was in awe every time that Molly Duncan took a solo. I had bought all his AWB records, and here was I sharing the same stage. Wow, life can still be good sometimes.

We started the second set with a storming version of 'Walkin the Dog'. The band really let loose with solos from Molly, Winston, Daniel, and Jose. This was funk/groove music at its best. Then Chantelle came on and we did a Motown medley of 'Dancin' in the Street', 'Just One Look', 'Stop in the Name of Love', and a great reggae version of Whitney Houston's 'I Will Always Love You'.

Everyone in the whole village was there, even the Mayor of the town. They all said it was the best music they had ever heard. We all felt quite chuffed at the performance with only a run through rehearsal, and we agreed it was definitely worth doing again if possible.

That whole weekend in Majorca was great. Those are the sorts of wonderful memories that you cherish, as they only happen once in a lifetime, and are usually never as good when you do it again.

Winston – Guitar/Vocals for Old Farts

Chris on Bass for The Old Farts

Molly and Me in Majorca for The Old Farts

Molly Duncan on stage with The Old Farts

Apprentice 'Old Fart' Brian Roberts (piano). He hasn't earned the Old Farts t-shirt yet (too young).

CHAPTER 13

Where Would We Be Without Friends?

Amazingly after going through a year from hell in 2002 fighting the 'Big C', one of the people that I received the most support from, other than my family and wonderful friends, were old Glasgow pal, Hamish Stuart, (ex Average White Band) who was really fantastic during that awful year. His regular e-mails with news of his tours and exciting gigs, and his words of comfort and support helped me get over all the emotional and mental rubbish you go through in the struggle to fight this awful illness, which is important, as all you feel like doing is crying with the pain most times. Ian Thomas (HSB/ Tom Jones drummer) was brilliant, as we had great talks on the phone with him telling me about all the people he had played with and the sessions he has done. Bass player, Steve Pearce, told me about the many years he spent as musical director for Tom

Jones, and all the great places he has played all over the world. Guitarist, Adam Philips, told me about the excellent sessions he has been on, one of them with Lionel Richie, which he said was fantastic. All the guys from Hamish's band were all great mates to me and so supportive.

The radiotherapy treatment affects you even a year later: I get very tired easily and find it hard to keep my spirits up. But with all my friends' support, plus my lovely family, things were looking decidedly better.

I had yet another surprise in 2002. Mark London, my old manager from Cartoone, got in contact. It was fantastic to talk to him after all these years. He was in hospital after an operation on his back, so he was feeling under the weather himself. I went to see Mark in hospital after 33 years. He looked so different from when I last saw him. He was much thinner with grey hair, but what an amazing guy. Mark gave me so much great advice on how to cope with everything, and as usual, his great sense of humour and personality made me laugh out loud. Mark always had a lot of knowledge about most things. Anything you wanted to talk about, Mark could usually form an opinion about it and speak with some authority on the subject. Mark was a tower of strength and support for me, always positive.

Mark and I never discussed what happened after Cartoone split up. All he said was that he was really sorry for me losing that wonderful drum kit and for not looking after me when Cartoone split, but it doesn't matter now as it was so long ago. He married Marion Massey, but they were divorced about 17 years ago. Mark now has another wife, Sabena, who he married about 12 years ago.

Jackie and I went out for a meal with Mike Allison and his wife Wendy, and also Derek's wife Gwynn and his son John Creigan. Mike told me about what he had been up to over the last 30 years since I saw him. He is now a granddad and enjoying life and keeping busy with his songwriting and recording duties for various people in the music industry.

So a lot had happened in 2002 with regard to the Cartoone story. People that I thought I would never see again, turned up out of the blue. Isn't life strange sometimes?

Ian Thomas (Drums), Pino Palladino (Bass)

Jim Mullen (Guitar), Hamish Stuart (Guitar)

360 Band at the 606 club, Chelsea. Featuring:
Molly Duncan, Steve Ferrone, Hamish Stuart.

Chapter 14

Good and Bad – What Can I Say?

2003 started off really badly with the shock of the sudden death of Maurice Gibb on 12th January 2003 from a heart attack due to surgery after cardiac arrest. I took Maurice's death very badly, as he was a fantastic bloke to be around from a personal point of view, forget that he was also a world class pop star. The thought that I would never see him again really hurt, as I was planning to go to Miami to see him after all these years. I wanted to know if he still had the tapes of Cartoone on *Top Of The Pops* and Lulu's Show as the BBC had wiped both shows and used the tapes again. So I was planning to go out there this year to touch base with him again. But now I will never get the chance to talk to him or spend time in his company ever again. I find that thought really sad, and after I heard the news, I couldn't sleep for days, and like everyone who loved Maurice, I played BeeGees records and videos over and over again. I just couldn't believe that he had gone. What a waste of such a lovely talented guy with so much to give.

Maurice was always so generous and such a down to earth type of guy, so easy to talk to with a wonderful sense of humour. I shall never forget the time I spent getting to know Maurice – memories I shall treasure forever. I read that a fan came up to him in his favourite restaurant in Miami and asked if he was '*the* Maurice Gibb'. It shows the measure of the man that not only did Maurice sit the guy down at his table to talk for half an hour, but took off his jacket, signed it 'All The Best From Maurice' on the inside, and gave it to him. What a guy. Maurice loved people and was so special and generous with his time.

I went to New York on Sunday 8th June 2003 to meet the Chairman of Atlantic Records, Ahmet Ertegun. He invited me over when he heard of my fight with the 'Big C'. So I was really looking forward to seeing him as he was nearly 80 years old now.

Monday 9th June 2003 was one of the best days of my life. I started the day with a beautiful shower, got dressed in what I thought were my casual but smart clothes, and then I went to a nice restaurant and had a lovely breakfast – great start to the day. I felt more alive than I have for ages. Phoned Jackie to tell her that I was okay and had a general chat telling her about my trip so far.

I had a wonderful time walking round New York in the blazing sunshine. Went to 'Manny's' the drum store and played on the electric drum kit they have there. I really enjoyed myself playing along to backing tracks, and then I went along to Atlantic Records to meet up with the Legendary Ahmet Ertegun. I wasn't feeling nervous, just excited to be meeting 'The Man' after all these years.

I was shown into his luxurious office by Francis, his excellent PA. Ahmet came into the office and I got up to shake his hand. He looked great for someone who is nearly 80 years old and was still immaculately dressed. He was as gracious and warm as I remembered him years ago. We talked for ages about the old times, and I asked him what had happened to all the people we knew. He told me that Jerry Wexler, after all this time, still sent him artists to listen too, but he only met up with Jerry about once a year for the Hall of Fame annual meeting.

Tom Dowd, one of the best record producers ever, died last year, which was a great loss to the world of music. Arif Mardin had semi-retired, but produced the record of the year 2002 by Nora Jones, and was awarded a Grammy in 2003 for producer of the year. So not many people left from the old days of the wonderful Atlantic Record Company headed by Ahmet and Jerry.

Only Ahmet was left from the people who remembered me and Cartoone. My, how time catches up with all of us. 34 years had passed like lightening. You don't realise how time goes slipping by without you noticing it.

An amazing coincidence happened while I was there. Jimmy Page released the three CD pack of Led Zeppelin live tracks and the DVD of all the Zeppelin live recordings. Both the CD and the DVD were number one in the USA while I was there in June 2003, and the last time I had met Ahmet 35 years ago in 1969, Led Zeppelin were number one with their debut album. Isn't that amazing?

We had some lunch and Ahmet told us a few funny stories of the old days at Atlantic. Then we took a few photos of myself with Ahmet, just for the memories of this wonderful day. All around his office there were pictures and notes from people like Mick Jagger, Phil Collins, and a lovely drawing of Ahmet by Tony Bennett. I gave Ahmet a picture of me signed 'Thanks For The Memories' which he loved, and put next to Mick Jagger's photo. This day will definitely go down as one of the highlights of my life – a wonderful special day meeting up again with a legend like Ahmet.

He told me something very interesting. He said

'We make sure that the artists we sign are between 18 years to 25 years, as that's the range we think they are most creative.' Also he said that 'Just because Cartoone didn't sell millions of records, it doesn't mean they weren't a great band, because they were. Atlantic Records would never have signed them otherwise.'

I have kept in touch with Ahmet since then, sending him emails and birthday/xmas cards etc. Francis his PA was always very sweet and kind, and made sure he got them all.

Ahmet Ertegun and me on 9ᵗʰ June 2003

After my meeting with Ahmet Ertegun, I went along to see my old buddy, Joey Helguara, who looked after the Atlantic Studio and produced all the Greatest Hits and re-release stuff from various Atlantic artists. Such a great guy with a brilliant sense of humour, he also plays guitar in his own blues band called King Dice. His wife, Amanda Moores, published her first book called

Grail Nights in 2016 which I hope is doing well for her.

I haven't seen Joey in years, but we do keep in touch by email every now and then. All the very best to you and Amanda for the future.

CHAPTER 15

Fletcher

My sons', Chris and Andy's, band Fletcher enjoyed touring the UK. They released an EP on 20th May 2002 with an independent record label, Deck Cheese Records. The CD sold really well for a first time out, and they got played every week on Radio 2. They also appeared live on the 'Lock-Up' show and played to 50,000 people at Finsbury Park in London, Deconstruction Festival 2002, where they opened the festival. This was also recorded and played on Radio 2 'The Lock-Up'.

They finished recording their debut album in April 2003, and it was released on 14 July 2003. It is called *My Revenge* and features 12 tracks by all of the band, including a track each from Olly (bass player) and Andy (drummer).

I think that it's so strong with very melodic catchy songs and power guitars to the fore, produced by ACE from punk band Skunk Anansie who had a few major hits in the 80's. I think it should have been a massive hit if there was any justice in this world.

Jackie and I are so grateful and proud of how our boys have turned out to be such lovely people, and a credit to themselves and us. God bless them and keep them safe and well.

Fletcher CD No24 in the Tower Records Chart

Chapter 16

2004 – Our Worst Year Yet

It was 20th January 2004 and there was something else lurking around the bend which we weren't aware of yet. Jackie and I got on with our lives, and tried to put the previous last few months behind us.

Things were getting back to normal once more, as we began to look to the future and have some degree of hope and renewed confidence that things were getting better. We had been through so much already and remained strong for each other and our boys. Surely we deserved a little break from all this fear and uncertainty about our future? Is there a God up there who looks out for us? Who knows? I hope so.

Wednesday 28th April 2004 and I was in Mr Sudderick's office once again. He was not happy about the small black thing at the back of my tongue. He had booked me in for a biopsy using a laser to take out the small lump at the back of my tongue on the 19th May 2004 (sounds worrying).

I got home to find that Ahmet Ertegun, the Chairman of Atlantic Records, had sent me a personal letter from him written on his own headed paper from Atlantic Records, wishing me and my family good wishes for the operation. He was so warm and caring to even send a letter to someone who was so low on the celebrity ladder. But that just shows the character of the man, and it made me feel very special. I will treasure it always along with my photo of us together.

19th May and my son, Chris, got me to the Mount Alvernia Hospital at 7 a.m. to book in for my operation. I was worried, but having Mr Sudderick doing the operation was something of a relief as he was the best of the best. The operation was a success and Mr Sudderick took the biopsy out of my tongue.

Wednesday the 26th May 2004 – Jackie and I went once again to see Mr Sudderick, and he told us that both biopsies tested positive for cancer. I must admit we were in total shock as I hadn't expected the cancer to come back again.

Mr Sudderick said that the lump he found at the back of my tongue was probably the 'Primary Cancer' they had been searching for in the last two years, but it was well hidden and didn't show itself until now. I would have to go in to have another operation on 11th June 2004 at the Nuffield Hospital to take the Primary cancer out. I was feeling pretty scared at this point, as I don't like the idea of having anything done inside my mouth.

The operation went well, I was told by Mr Sudderick, and he was pleased that the nerves in my mouth area hadn't seized up due to the surgery (it was a risk). I was feeling absolutely out of it, and had all sorts of tubes and stuff coming out of me. I didn't like the oxygen mask, but was told by the nurse that it was essential I keep it on.

The next day I was so pleased that I was able to still speak, even with a slight lisp. At least I could talk which was something to be thankful for. Mr Sudderick kept me in for one more day and said that I was fine to go home, and told me to take things easy.

Wednesday 23rd June 2004 – back in Mr Sudderick's office to hear the results of the operation and extra biopsies he had taken. All the biopsies were clear except one. This meant that Mr Sudderick would have to take some more off my tongue as the cancer was still there. What do I say to that? My god, not another operation! And he wanted to do it this Friday, 25th Jun 2004, which was only two days away.

'Jeez, how will I get through all this stuff?' I thought as he told me, 'but I must try and be strong for the sake of my family and all the people who care about me.'

Friday 25th June 2004 – Chris took me to the Mount Alvernia Hospital in Guildford for 7 a.m. to book in for the operation. I felt nervous about the operation, but tried not to show it, as I had every confidence in my surgeon Mr Sudderick, and I knew he would look after me. The operation took seven hours this time as Mr Sudderick took the lump out plus 60 lymph nodes, just to make sure he caught it all ('belt and braces' he called it). I was feeling absolutely exhausted when I came round after the operation, and drifted in and out of sleep every time this machine automatically took my blood pressure, as it had dropped dramatically, and they were worried, so they told me afterwards.

I was so tired and sore when I came round from it. Mr Sudderick told me that he'd had to take a third of my tongue away to ensure that he got all the cancer cells this time.

I came out of hospital on Saturday 3rd July 2004, and my middle son, Andy, picked me up. God I was feeling like hell and my mouth felt like it didn't belong to me. The scar on my neck ran from my left ear down the front of my neck to the right ear, and because he had used giant staples my neck felt like it was in a brace – very tight indeed. But at least I was alive to tell the tale – that's something to be thankful for.

It was Jackie's birthday and we went to see Mr Sudderick to hear the results of the operation and to take the staples out. Of all the 60 lymph nodes he took out, only one was cancerous and that was gone so it looked good. I took Jackie to Little Italy in Kingston so her sons could make a fuss of her and they gave their mum some nice presents. So all in all it turned out to be a good day.

Wednesday 14th July 2004 – back in Mr Sudderick's office, but this time he had my Oncologist with him Dr. Stephen Whitaker, who told me that I would have to undergo eight weeks of radiotherapy to my face and neck.

Monday 2nd August 2004 was one of my days from hell. I had to be fitted for a mask so that I could undergo the radiotherapy. I endured the plaster covering my whole face with just a hole for my nose to breathe through, as I knew it was important. I went back to the hospital to have the mask verification and fitting on Monday 16th August 2004. I got to the hospital and they put the finished mask on me. From experience of the last time I had radiotherapy I knew what to expect. There was no way I could wear that mask for half an hour with just holes for my nose, as I can't bear anything covering my face. I asked the chap to cut more holes into it. He said that he couldn't without having the green light from my Consultant.

So I had to get dressed again and go upstairs to see my Consultant, Dr. Stephen Whitaker. I told him that they either cut some more holes into the mask or I was determined not to go through with the radiotherapy.

Finally after seeing how serious I was, he agreed to the mask being cut. I went back downstairs and they cut the mask how I wanted it, so I was able to go into the CT Scan and the Simulator wearing the mask. They measured and marked the mask up with all the points that they would be targeting with the laser, I was now ready for my radiotherapy treatment.

I won't bore you with all the gory details other than to say that the first two weeks were alright, but after that it got steadily worse, as I started to have trouble with my mouth and throat which they were hammering with radiation every day, and it became very sore and difficult to swallow. Plus I developed this awful mucus where I just couldn't stop bringing up mucus and spitting it out. I did this constantly for 24 hours a day. I filled carrier bags full of tissues from the mucus – it was absolute hell. Then, as I got near to the end of the treatment, my earlobe split open and was bleeding and raw due to the path they were hitting. It got so painful and bad they had to stop the radiation for two days to allow me to heal.

Somehow I managed to get through this nightmare, even though my beloved moustache fell off, to my horror. I'd had it for 35 years and felt naked without my moustache. I was so miserable, but didn't realise at the time that it would get much worse before it got better. I had so much trouble with my mouth and throat that I couldn't taste or swallow anything properly without a drink to wash it down, as my mouth would just dry up with no saliva. My lips would stick to my teeth, so I couldn't speak properly either.

Then I developed the terrible headaches and jaw-aches, which to my mind were much worse than migraines. I had liquid morphine to take every four hours, but the morphine would only work for two hours, so you had two hours in pain before you could take another hit of morphine. After a while I got some sleep but not much. I was living on special drinks to keep me from dehydrating, and lost at least 5 stone (70 lbs).

I would just lie there in pain for hours, as day went into night and it didn't really matter as I was so out of it by then. I had about ten mouth ulcers due to thrush in my mouth. I don't know how I managed to cope with it all, but somehow I got the strength to get through just one day at a time, and got better with each passing day.

All through this terrible traumatic period, the Inland Revenue kept chasing me for money. They worked out that they hadn't charged me enough tax when I filled out my tax return online, so they went back another five years and charged me thousands. They even sent me a notice for £900 the day before one of my major operations. If I didn't pay it immediately, they would charge interest daily. My wife went to the bank that day and paid it. It's true what they say, 'There are three things that are certain in life: you're born, you die, and you pay your taxes' (unless you're rich and can afford a good accountant).

Before my four operations, I phoned the tax office to inform them that I was having treatment for cancer and to please leave me alone until after I had recovered. I would sort everything out then. I suppose they just treat it as a job and don't think about the person they are sending the bills to or how it affects them.

It's amazing the inner strength we have within us all to get us through such nightmares. I suppose you either fight or give up: there are only two options. I couldn't give up because of all the looks on the faces of my family willing me to keep on fighting. Looking back at how bad I really was, I don't know how I managed to get through it.

Robert Sudderick and Stephen Whitaker, the two men who have kept me alive over the last 17 years. Thank you guys.

Me with Dr. Whitaker's PA, Anne, and Mr Sudderick's PA, Judith, my guardian angel.

CHAPTER 17

A New Beginning

2005 had been alright so far. I had gone to visit Mark London and his lovely wife Sabena. Mark was still writing songs which I was glad to hear, as he is a wonderful songwriter. I wish I could have written such a brilliant song as 'To Sir With Love' as it will always be a classic. The film starred Sidney Poitier in the lead role, and Lulu had an excellent part in it also. Mark was still an amazing personality, with great knowledge and passion for life. He was a constant source of support to me, as whenever I felt a bit low, I just phoned Mark and he'd give me a swift kick up the backside, and tell me to get on with my life and not waste time worrying over what might be. It stopped me feeling sorry for myself, and helped me get the right perspective into my life.

I was back at work now, mainly part time, just so I could get used to the journey into work, and also being back in the office environment again was very strange. Lots of pain still from my muscles growing back due to the fact that when I couldn't eat anything my body ate itself in a manner of speaking. Now that I was eating again my muscles were growing back, but it was very painful. Still no taste in anything I ate. There are two types of tastes that I was told about that are caused by radiotherapy, one is 'metal' and the other is 'cardboard'. Thankfully I have the latter, as I couldn't bear to have all my food taste of metal – that would be awful.

Every day was a gift really, as I didn't know how long I had left. I tried to make each day a good one, but as Jackie said, I went round as if the whole world was on my shoulders. Sometimes it certainly seemed that way to me. But I had to appreciate how far I had come since last year, and not wallow in my own problems. I just took each day at a time and didn't worry about tomorrow so much.

Andy on drums at the London Astoria

Me and Mark London when I visited him and wife, Sabena

Chris on Guitar/Vocals at London Astoria

Chapter 18

I Meet Dennis Sheehan at Long Last

On 18th–19th June 2005 I finally got to meet Dennis Sheehan at the U2 concert at Twickenham Rugby Stadium. I was so looking forward to seeing Dennis after all these years, plus hoping to meet the legendary U2, especially Bono who was in the news constantly at the time. He seemed a really interesting guy.

It was Saturday 18th June 2005 and Jackie dropped me off at Twickenham Stadium where the mighty U2 were playing two sold out nights. I felt really excited about actually meeting Dennis Sheehan after all these years. I hoped he would recognise me. I reached the VIP entrance where Dennis told me to wait. He recognised me straight way, as he called my name. Dennis had changed so much (it has been 36 years). He had white hair now and had obviously put on a bit of weight as you do when you get to our age, but I did recognise him. He gave me a big hug and a pass that said U2 'Working' on it, so I took off the back and stuck it on my shirt.

Dennis took me into his tour manager's room where I met all his many staff. The U2 tour staff is run like a super efficient army, with each 'regiment' doing their part for the bigger picture. I suppose they are split into the Stage Crew, Sound Crew and Road Crew who drive all the trucks with the equipment to each new stadium for the next gig. Dennis would be the head 'General' in charge of the admin staff, coordinating all his colonels. Looking at all the equipment and massive stage, plus all the amps and instruments for the group U2, it is just awesome how they can pack it all away and have it set up again in another part of the UK only two days later. Wow. Amazing.

I am so impressed by the sheer size of the organisation and how everything and everybody seemed to know their jobs, and get on with it just like a well oiled machine. I suppose they had done this so many times they had got to know the best way of doing it with the smallest amount of fuss.

Unfortunately I didn't have much time with Dennis due to his U2 duties. He said that his busiest times were in London, Paris, Dublin, Los Angeles, so he didn't have much spare time to spend with me. Dennis took me up to the mixing desk, which was in the middle of Twickenham Rugby Stadium, and the VIP area. I recognised a few famous faces there – the place where I was standing near the mixing desk. A group of people saw my pass and asked me what 'Work' I was doing for U2. Not knowing what to say, I jokingly said that I was responsible for Bono's sunglasses, and I had to make sure that he had the right pair on that suited the song.

As luck would have it, Bono came out on stage just then, and had changed from the yellow glasses to the all black glasses. The whole group of people turned round and said, 'Good Job –Man'. I had to really hold myself back from laughing out loud, as they actually believed me. The gig was absolutely amazing with U2 playing a storming set and 77,000 people cheering every single song. There were many highlights, but when Bono sang 'I Still Haven't Found What I'm Looking For' and he told the band to play quiet, the whole stadium sang the chorus over and over again – 77,000 people singing in one voice (in tune). The whole atmosphere was electric, and Bono was suitably impressed with the audience.

A brilliant night – I saw U2 play and I got to meet my old mate Dennis Sheehan as well. It just shows the character of the man. Dennis only text me a couple days later to say how sorry he was that we didn't have more time to spend together, and that he would keep in touch. If that was anybody else then I wouldn't have expected to hear from him again, but Dennis was an excellent guy who I knew would get in touch when he got the time. He was a man of his word, which is hard to find these days, in a world full of selfish shallow music business people who only speak to you to network, hoping they can get free tickets to gigs or get asked backstage to the VIP area where they can mix with other shallow people like themselves. I think the expression is 'freeloaders'.

Dennis Sheehan came to visit me and Jackie on the 15th November 2009. It was a bit of a shock at first, as it was totally unexpected, but very welcome. He was in the area and thought he would drop in for a few hours to catch up with old times. What a pleasant but lovely surprise. He is such a lovely guy. Jackie and I really enjoyed his company, and we talked for ages about everything that had happened to us and also our plans for the future. We asked him about looking after U2 – was it very stressful?

Dennis was very diplomatic and said, 'The good stuff by far outweighs the bad stuff' and that's all he would say about it – superb loyalty from Dennis as always. I hoped to see him again soon.

My U2 Vertigo Access Pass

Dennis and his U2 Staff at Twickenham Rugby Stadium

*Dennis and me in 1969 when I was living
with him and his wife, Lisa, in Ealing*

CHAPTER 19

Time To Make A Choice

Wednesday 11th July 2007 – Back full circle in Robert Sudderick's office to be told that the biopsies he took the week before were positive and the cancer had come back, in my Larynx/Vocal Chords this time.

He told my wife Jackie and I that due to all the treatment I'd had previously, they wouldn't consider radio or chemotherapy, and the only option left would be surgery to my voice box (larynx). This was a major operation with serious consequences to my quality of life. At this moment in time I dreaded the thought of going through all that pain and really bad discomfort in breathing etc. that comes after the operation. The option to not have the operation would mean that I would be dead in less than three months due to the dangerous position of the cancer, as the cancer would grow over my windpipe and choke me. So I didn't really have a choice other than to go through with it.

It's funny how life turns out, as on the Friday 13th July 2007 I was in despair in the morning as I had received an e-mail from a person who had the larynx operation, and it really brought it all home to me. It suddenly sunk in what it all meant to lose your voice box and the devastating effect it would have on my future life. I cried my eyes out for the first time in years, and once I let go I couldn't stop crying for hours. I went through the whole 'Why me?' scenario, and cursed god for giving me back the cancer in such a dangerous place that my only option was surgery. After I had exhausted myself crying, I just sat there on the sofa and just stared at the wall in a state of pure doom and gloom. I had lost all hope of a future in which I could ever be happy again.

Just then my Jackie came home from work and told me she had some news for me. Jackie told me that she had been on the phone to my consultants for the past few days begging them to try something else other than surgery. She said that secretly my wonderful sons had pooled their money together and paid for a trip to Las Vegas for my 60th birthday, and they didn't want to cancel as I probably wouldn't be able to go after the operation.

Jackie said my consultants had worked out a plan to help me go on my trip to Las Vegas. The only thing was I would have to endure six days of intensive 24 hour chemotherapy and all the possible after effects. I, of course, said yes, as I wanted to go on the trip with my boys, so I would have done anything to make that happen. When Jackie told me, the relief I felt that I wouldn't be having the operation until I got back from Vegas (stay of execution) and to know that my wonderful family had paid for a trip of a lifetime for me to go to Las Vegas for my 60th Birthday – I couldn't believe how the day had turned out. After all the despair and heartache of the morning, to have this amazing news in the afternoon from my Jackie was awesome. What a woman she is. That's what you call unselfish real love, and I'm blessed to have her as my wife. How lucky am I?

I was helped through the chemotherapy by none other than Mike Allison, who phoned me every single day whilst I was in hospital. He was brilliant and supportive, talking about Las Vegas, telling me about when he went there for his son, Stephen's, wedding, giving me advice on places to visit etc. We talked about what happened after Cartoone split, and what we did in all those years we didn't see each other. Mike was amazingly kind and thoughtful, as I was feeling very fragile, and I won't forget him for that. They sent me home after six days of 24 hour intense chemo being pumped into me. The first day home I felt ill, but carried on regardless. As the day passed I got more and more ill. Monday I felt very sick but didn't know whether to phone the hospital or not. But on the Tuesday I woke up with a very badly swollen face and neck, loads of mouth ulcers, and terrible pains in my head and ears with a temperature of 39.9C which is very high. I knew something wasn't right, and asked Jackie to phone the hospital. They said to bring me in immediately. Jackie managed to get me into her little car, and she drove me back to the hospital. On arrival, I was delirious and just kept feeling worse and worse. They immediately admitted me onto the ward, and the doctor was on hand to assess me.

The next three days, I was hallucinating and they kept putting antibiotics and other medication intravenously to try and bring the fever down. My blood count of white blood cells was zero, which meant that I had virtually no immune system at all. They injected me in the stomach with white blood cell boosters to try and help my immune system. It was only by Friday that I began to rally and my blood count started to rise once again to 1.75 which was better than zero.

Back home again after two weeks in hospital, I was feeling much better, and ready to begin my fight to get fit for the Las Vegas trip with my three amazing sons. The next two weeks were absolute hell, as I was so weak and tired all the time. I force fed myself to try and get my strength up so I could go with my sons to Vegas.

Chapter 20

The Las Vegas Road Trip

I had managed to get myself strong enough to make the long journey to Las Vegas with my sons. I was still feeling a bit under the weather, but the excitement of the holiday overcame all the minor problems. We were flying from Heathrow on American Airlines via Chicago. It would be the first time I had been in Chicago since touring there with Cartoone in 1969.

Our trip to Las Vegas was eventful, as expected. With all the security at Heathrow, it took a long time to get through the checks etc., but once on the plane we enjoyed the flight. I watched a couple of films and the boys played video games on their Nintendo DSs until we got to Chicago. We lined up at US Customs and the officer booked us into the USA. Matt was picked at random to go through a proper check of his baggage etc., which was fine as we didn't bring much with us anyway. The flight from Chicago to Las Vegas was delayed and we had to sit in the plane on the runway waiting for a storm to pass over before we could take off. It took about an hour to pass over, and when it did, we had never seen such rain. It was so fast and heavy we couldn't see the other planes on the runway until it had passed over. So not a good start to our flight to Las Vegas, but as we got closer to the west coast, the weather brightened up and sun came out.

We arrived in Las Vegas in a heat wave of 34 degrees, and it hit us the moment we got off the plane – wonderful to feel that heat on our bodies after the cold and wet of Chicago. We hailed a cab to take us to our hotel, Sam's Town, on the outskirts of the strip. We loved the hotel, as it had everything we needed, and the rooms were nice and comfortable, plus the price was reasonable too. As we drove to our hotel, the cab driver took us down the Vegas strip. It was really exciting to see and actually be there at last, even though we felt jetlagged and tired. Plus it was Andy's birthday and we wanted to celebrate it, so we went to a really nice restaurant and had a steak dinner with all the trimmings. Then we just sat in a bar, relaxed and watched a show. I was feeling great to be in Vegas with my wonderful special sons. I felt a bit rough after the flight, but I didn't let my sons see it, as I didn't want to spoil their fun. We planned the whole itinerary of our holiday, so we wouldn't waste any time doing silly things.

On the Saturday, my 60th birthday, I woke up and the boys called me into their room at the hotel. They had got up early and gone out and bought balloons and a cake with candles. I was so chuffed, and had forgotten it was my birthday, so it was a genuine surprise to me. We drove to the Grand Canyon with Chris taking over the driving duties as he had been there before. Five hours of driving – we passed the Hoover Dam, and some other great sites on the way. With the sun shining and the music playing on the excellent radio station we had found, we were having a great time singing along to all the songs. The sky was a beautiful blue with hardly any clouds.

We took this track which said Grand Canyon, and we had to travel 35 miles on this bloody dusty old road, and we couldn't get a signal on our mobile phones, so we were hoping that we didn't break down, otherwise we would be stuffed.

When we got to the Grand Canyon it was an awesome sight. You have to be there to appreciate it as no film or photo does it justice. We sat there all together on these rocks on the edge of the canyon just looking and taking in the sights of the

Colorado river and the sheer size of the Grand Canyon. After an hour or so the boys just said, 'Happy Birthday Dad. You made it' and the tears of pure emotion were streaming down my face with happiness and the fact that me and my lovely sons were all able to share this together. I will treasure that moment forever.

Every day was a pleasure with my sons. We were all very relaxed and chilled out, as there was no time frame or schedule to get to. We just did all the usual tourist stuff, visiting all the hotels and playing Blackjack in all of them. Some we won, some we lost; it all balanced out in the end, and we had a fantastic time trying our luck on all the tables. I wore my cowboy hat at the tables, but they wouldn't let us take any pictures in the casinos, so I never got a photo of me with my boys playing Blackjack looking like Clint Eastwood.

We ate at some great restaurants, and the food was excellent and their portions were massive. I couldn't finish it, but the boys ate well with some big steaks being devoured.

We played ten pin bowling at 1.30 a.m. in the morning. It was nice and relaxed and so enjoyable having a laugh with my sons.

Andy was very brave, as we went up to the Stratosphere Hotel where you can get an amazing view of Las Vegas from 350m up, and Andy decided to go on this ride at the top of the Stratosphere. His face when he came down after the ride was a picture, as all the colour had gone. He said, with a big grin, that it was so scary because you were so high up and it was outside, so you felt the rush of the wind in your face as the ride shot up in the air, and then came crashing down again.

I can't thank my sons enough for taking me to Las Vegas. It was always my dream to go there and also to go to the Grand Canyon. But I didn't realise how ill I was until we went to the Luxor Hotel, and they had this special photo shop where they superimpose your face onto the body of your hero film star. So I chose to be Sean Connery as James Bond, and it was only when he showed me the photo of my face on Sean's body did I see just how ill I really looked. My eyes were sunken and all my hair had fallen out including my eyebrows due to all the chemotherapy treatment. I just took one look and said no thank you to the guy, as I had never seen myself looking so bad.

We managed to see The Beatles show, *LOVE*, in

the Mirage Hotel. It was an amazing show with the music from The Beatles specially produced by George Martin for the show.

It was a trip of a lifetime for me and the boys in sunny Las Vegas, Nevada, and we were all happy on our way to the airport to take the journey back to the UK. All the way back on the journey, I couldn't stop thinking about what lay ahead the next day after I got to the UK. I was devastated at the thought of losing my voice forever. I'd had that voice for 60 years and I loved it.

I didn't want the journey to end, and I didn't want to face the operation to take away my voice. I was always singing to myself and loved the old karaoke where I could do my impression of Tom Jones. Now that they were taking it away, I appreciated what I was losing and dreaded every minute that brought me closer to that eventuality.

Matt and me in the Nevada Desert USA

Andy and Chris in the Nevada Desert USA

L-R: Andy, Chris, me and Matt outside Vegas Airport

*Matt and me on his Graduation Day – Matt got
a degree in Music which I am so proud of.*

168

This is me on my 60th Birthday in Las Vegas with my son Chris. Five days after this photo was taken, I had my operation to take away my voice forever.

CHAPTER 21

The Day I Lost My Voice/ Vocal Chords Forever

1ˢᵗ September 2007 – My only comfort is that Robert Sudderick was the surgeon carrying out my operation. I had every confidence in that man, and knew he would look after me.

My oldest son, Chris, and my wife, Jackie, took me to the hospital for moral support. I was dreading the operation and didn't know how I would cope with the after effects of it. On the plane home from Las Vegas I'd had plenty of time to think, and my heart said yes to the operation, but my head said no. I really didn't want to go through life with whatever time I had left being pitied by people because of my new circumstances of being without a voice box, and talking through a 'valve' with a croaky artificial voice.

I actually seriously considered just letting the cancer take its course and eventually choke me to death. Mr Sudderick told me that if I didn't have the operation, I would be dead within three months, due to where the cancer was in my larynx. The thought of having to breathe out of a large hole in my neck, and waking up after the operation and not being able to make a sound scared the hell out of me. The fact that I was 60 years old and had achieved most of which I was going to do in my life, I was quite prepared to let go and give in or give up, whichever way you want to look at it. But the looks on my family's faces made me want to fight to survive to be around for them, as they do love me and want me around. So I agreed to go through with the operation for the sake of my family and all the people who care about me.

On a completely selfish note, my quality of life being a laryngectomee would change drastically: the way people viewed me and the way I viewed myself. I imagined my self esteem would drop through the floor. I used to think I was this tough Scotsman with a fighting spirit, as I had fought through the cancer twice already, but now I was feeling weak and vulnerable. They told me that, after the operation, I would be in the intensive care ward for two days while I came round post-op, so Jackie and I agreed that she wouldn't come and see me until the second night.

2nd September – I was coming in and out of consciousness and kept hearing the sound of air very loudly as it was pumped into the new hole in my neck. I vaguely remember Mr Sudderick coming to see me saying that the operation was a success, and he had cut away all the cancer along with my voice box and vocal chords. I was half asleep but managed to write the words 'Thank you' on a writing pad and then fell back to sleep.

Jackie and Marissa, my daughter-in-law, came to see me and sat either side of the bed and held my hand. I shall always remember how comforting that moment felt when I woke up and saw them both there. I needed it so badly as I was feeling very fragile.

After two days and nights in intensive care, I was moved into a normal room on the ward, and looked after by some wonderful nurses on a 24/7 basis. I couldn't bear to look at the hole in my neck, with a tube coming out of my chest which was used to feed me with. The nurses changed this bag of what looked like brown porridge and I could feel it going through the tube into my stomach – it felt really weird. The thought of a large open hole in my neck where you could look into my throat made me feel quite sick. I could easily tell lies and say it didn't bother me at all and act all tough, but the truth is it was a big thing to get used to.

I was in the hospital for two weeks, and was looked after superbly. I was allowed home after I could eat solids like scrambled egg, jelly and ice cream unaided. They then took out the feeding tube and sent me home for Jackie to look after me. She did a wonderful job cleaning out my hole (stoma) with all the horrible mucus that had gathered there. Slowly but surely, I got stronger each day and started to eat proper food such as spaghetti, which I found easy to swallow. I even began to put on a bit of weight.

The following ten months were the hardest for me mentally and emotionally. Trying to get used to all the changes and also having to accept the way it was now. Every day was a struggle, but I never gave up, and made great leaps in my recovery. After three months of silence and having to write everything down, not able to make a sound, I was finally able to speak through an artificial plastic valve and make a 'voice' that was very croaky, but still kept my accent. Hamish Stuart said that because I couldn't say my 'H's' but spoke with a Scottish accent, I was a new species: a 'Jockney'. I thought it described me perfectly.

CHAPTER 22

Letter To Richard Desmond
- *Owner of OK Magazine/Daily Express/ Health Lottery*

I was wondering what to do with myself now that I wasn't working anymore. I wanted to do something for charity and thought of a great idea, so wrote an email to Richard Desmond, the owner of *OK Magazine* and *The Daily Express* about it.

The idea came after I saw the film *The Bucket List* with Jack Nicholson and Morgan Freeman. The idea was to have a ' Musical Bucket List' where I would play one song with the artists on the list before I kicked the bucket, and they in turn would give money to the cancer charities that I would represent. Obviously I wouldn't be able to kick the bucket until I had played with all the artists on my list, so it could go on for years, as it would give me the incentive to live until I had fulfilled my dream project.

After my email, Richard said it was impossible, but didn't give the reasons why. Richard felt bad that he couldn't make it work for me, so he sent Jackie and me a VIP invite to the *OK Magazine* Summer Party to mix with all the celebrities and have fun. Not to be put off, I wrote to all the main Cancer charities, and they came back with the same answer 'It's impossible, and wouldn't work' but they also didn't give the reason.

It suddenly dawned on me that the reason it wouldn't work, and why they didn't tell me, is that I'm 'Charlie Nobody', an old and passed it, has-been drummer who nobody has heard of.

Now if my name was Ringo Starr then it would be a different story, as he is the most famous drummer in the world, and I'm sure everyone would be fighting over his Musical Bucket List.

So I got the message in the end and gave up on my quest to do my Musical Bucket List.

Here is the review I sent Richard Desmond:

We were invited by Richard Desmond to a special VIP Summer Party for OK Magazine on Sunday 15th June 2008 at the Excel, London.

It was really exciting being amongst all the rich and famous celebrities, as everyone you have known from TV was there. My wife Jackie and I had such a laugh playing 'Spot the Celeb'. We recognised so many faces, but couldn't remember all their names. I had to laugh as one the celebs from 'Loose Women' came over to our table to eat her food, and Jackie recognised her straight away, said hello and chatted to her quite naturally. It was so well *organised, so much food and champagne being brought around by attentive waiters and waitresses. All the celebs have a fantastic life going to these functions.*

All the editors of OK magazine from all over the world were introduced on stage by TV presenter, Tania Bryer. She also did a great job of introducing the RD Crusaders onstage. You could feel the buzz of excitement in the air as all the celebs were walking round posing for OK's photographers, and everyone was looking forward to the concert with great anticipation.

The organisers took away everybody's cameras and mobile phones so we couldn't take photos of the celebs. Then at the end sold them back to us for a donation to Teenage Cancer Trust (nice touch).

The day finished with a special concert by the RD Crusaders, the band Richard Desmond, the owner of OK and Daily Express, put together for Teenage Cancer Trust.

The band members were as follows:-

Drums: Richard Desmond (drummer and number one charity Crusader – £18 million so far)

Lead Guitar: Russ Ballard (Argent)

Rhythm Guitar: Steve Townsend (The Who)

Keyboards: Zoot Money

Bass Guitar: Rick Willis (Foreigner and Bad Company)

Keyboards: Steve Smith

Lead Singers: The legendary Lulu, Steve Harley (Cockney Rebel), Peter Andre, Robert Hart (Bad Company)

Backing Singers: Steve Balselmo, Jackie Rawe

The concert was amazing with all the old soul stuff coming out from Peter Andre who was brilliant. Steve Harley sang his anthem 'Come Up and See Me, Make Me Smile' and the whole crowd sang along. Russ Ballard sang his classic song from Argent, 'Hold Your Head Up', to thunderous applause, and Jackie

Rawe did a storming version of 'Knock On Wood' that really grooved with great phrasing on the vocal.

The best was saved for last as Lulu absolutely stole the show with her first song: a blistering 'I'll Go Crazy'. She was on the floor kneeling and passionately pleading with the audience as she sang the song. Lulu really knows how to work the crowd as she sang a funky version of 'I Can't Turn You Loose', the old Otis Redding classic. Lulu finished her set with 'Shout', her hit from the 60s, and the crowd all sang along – what a voice, what a performer. Awesome!

Robert Hart did a sterling job of all the rock songs like 'Pinball Wizard' and 'Can't Get Enough Of Your Love'. He had a really powerful voice, perfect for those full on throaty songs. Richard Desmond was rock solid on drums throughout, having to play loads of different styles within the set list. He was the foundation of the band that glued everything together. Richard's Ludwig drum kit sounded great. The bass drum and tom-toms had a nice deep punch to them and the snare drum had a lovely 'crack' to it that cut through the sound of the band easily. Well done the sound mixing desk guys.

The show finished with a medley of all the old soul classics from Lulu, Robert Hart, and Peter Andre:

'What Becomes of the Brokenhearted', 'Signed Sealed Delivered', 'Reach Out', 'Same Old Song', etc. etc. It was a great show put on by a great band for charity The Teenage Cancer Trust.

Jackie and I had an amazing, enjoyable day we will never forget. Thank you Richard Desmond and OK Magazine.

Jackie and me (top right) in OK VIP Magazine

CHAPTER 23

2008 – A Year of Joy and Pain

In September, Jackie and I celebrated our 37th wedding anniversary. Looking back over all those years, I couldn't have wished for anyone other than my Jackie to share it with. She has been an amazing wife and friend to me, and I'm so grateful and lucky to be married to her.

Also we celebrated a year since my laryngectomy operation and still being around to tell the tale, although it has been a hard struggle emotionally and mentally having to adjust to breathing out of a hole in my neck, and getting used to talking with my new artificial valve. Some people have been very compassionate and treated me well while others have been scared by my voice and me having to press my neck to speak, but once they get used to it, it's not so bad. So, slowly but surely, I have adjusted to my new circumstances, and the fact that I'm still alive is a bonus.

My sons took me to see Stevie Wonder play at the O2 arena. Chris and Jett had really good seats, but Andy and I were at the back of the hall. We could see okay, but tended to look at the big screens as Stevie looked too far away onstage, but the music was fantastic, and he had a great band, so it was worth going to see him play live at the O2 arena. But I paid the price of mixing with 20,000 people at the concert and breathing in all their germs. The next day I woke up to find that my throat was sore and my chest was very painful. Obviously I had caught an infection from mixing at the concert, as I basically have no protection through the hole in my neck. It took two weeks and loads of antibiotics to finally get rid of the infection, so I realised that I had to be careful about mixing with large crowds of people from now on. The main thing was that I did enjoy the concert with the wonderful, legendary Stevie Wonder. Stevie was fantastic and his band were amazingly tight and so funky.

Goodbye Wonderful Lucy – 8th December 2008

Goodbye wonderful Lucy. You were the most special dog anyone could wish for.

To Chris, Andy and Matt, you were their playmate, and you had so much fun and laughter over the years with them. I'm sure they all have their own personal memories of the joy that Lucy brought into their lives.

To your mum, Jackie, you were her little white angel with a special bond between you that went deep into her soul.

Lucy you were such a character and an actress with a fantastic personality. Those big eyes told everything you were feeling and wanted to express. Always so proud and dignified to the end, you were a real lady.

To me you were my constant companion, always there giving so much love and comfort in abundance without end.

I did everything for you, and you loved me for it, I know that for sure. You will forever be in my heart and my soul, and if there is a doggy heaven then I hope you are happy there running in the fields and the lakes.

Life is full of Joy and Pain. We celebrate the Joy of having our dear Lucy in our lives for so long, as she brought us so much pleasure. We endure the Pain of losing her, and we all miss her dearly each and every day.

Never to be forgotten, bless you darling Lucy.

Lucy on her chair relaxing – so gorgeous

CHAPTER 24

40 Year Anniversary for Cartoone – 2009

2009 would mark 40 years since Ahmet Ertegan signed Cartoone to Atlantic Records and released their debut album featuring Jimmy Page on guitar.

To celebrate this anniversary, Dave Kapp from Rhino Records (Atlantic) re-released Cartoone's original album as a download on Tuesday 7th April 2009 on iTunes.

On the 7th April 2009, I downloaded Cartoone from iTunes. The only sad thing is there is no money in the pot for promoting the album, which is a crying shame. But it would cost a small fortune to advertise it properly on the web, and I don't think that Rhino will pay that sort of money for an old 60s band, even if Jimmy Page is on the album.

So for drastic measures I went to every site and forum I could find and put a message on it about the

Cartoone re-release, but I didn't feel confident, as it would only reach a few hundred people. We needed to reach millions to have any chance of it selling.

Friday Music released the album on CD, with the second album as bonus tracks on Tuesday 9th June 2009. Joe Reagoso from Friday Music contacted me, and I sent him a load of photos and some anecdotes from that period to go on the liner notes for the album. Dave Kapp from Rhino Records gave Joe the original 'Master Tapes' of Cartoone, and permission to go ahead and re-mix it for the Cartoone Deluxe Edition CD. It was a labour of love for both myself and Joe, but worth it.

Mike and I did an interview for US radio shows, *Carol Miller Show* and *Get The Led Out* which is a Led Zeppelin radio show that goes out coast to coast in USA, but I don't think it was ever broadcast – such a shame.

Have a look at the Friday Music website and see the write up that Joe Reagoso did on the webpage – it's great. While you're there, you could maybe buy the Cartoone Deluxe Edition CD.

www.fridaymusic.com

CHAPTER 25

My Mum is Rushed to Hospital

On the 27th July 2009 my Mum went into Queen's Hospital in Romford with lumps all over her body, her right eye all swollen, and a lump at the back of her head. It took one and a half weeks to do a biopsy on her to find out what was wrong. The doctor said it was the surgeon to blame as he was so busy with emergencies that my mum's biopsy took a back seat and went to the bottom of the list. My wife, Jackie, asked the doctor if it was because my mum was old (84 years) that they were putting her case to the bottom of the list as they didn't want to spend any NHS money on trying to diagnose and possibly save my mum's life and saw it as waste of money, but the doctor didn't answer.

After six weeks of living hell laying in bed in pain and terrible discomfort, my mum's weight dropped to around five stone, and still they did nothing. But now they were saying she had terminal cancer of the lungs and bones. They were now talking about a hospice and palliative care. What a nightmare for my poor mum. She had been so brave and strong, at least in front of us anyway. My mum said it was awful at night, as loads of patients were pressing their buzzers, but nobody came to them.

On the fifth week that Jackie and I visited my mum, she was looking awful, and deteriorating fast. My sister, Linda, and her partner, John, stayed in Mum's bungalow and visited every day, and kept me up to date. We spoke to the Macmillan nurse, and she said my mum was very poorly and they were keeping her pain free and as comfortable as possible. I asked her how long my mum had, and she said two weeks at most.

In what turned out to be the last time I would see my mum alive, she allowed me to fuss with her, stroke her hair and hold hands, something she never ever did, as my mum wasn't one for showing any affection or touching, I don't remember her cuddling me. It would always be me giving her a cuddle. As Jackie and I left she said, 'I love it when you and Jackie visit me, as you never interrupt me when I'm speaking.' That was my mum's sense of humour, very tongue in cheek but true, as she loved to talk.

On Friday 4th September 2009 at 7 a.m., my Mum finally passed away peacefully in her sleep. At 8 a.m. the next day, BBC Radio 2's Brian Matthew played Cartoone's song 'Girl Of Yesterday', my mum's favourite song on his show *Sound Of The 60s*. Was this a sign from my mum, as it's been 40 years since Cartoone were on UK radio, and you would have thought that they would play 'Penny For The Sun' our single, but no, they played my mum's favourite track from the album. That is really spooky, and you have to admit it is a million to one chance of that ever happening. Was it a sign from her to say she is alright now and at peace, or was it just a happy coincidence? We will never know. That is why we played it at her funeral on Friday 11th September 2009, to celebrate her life and send her off with her favourite song.

We had the funeral in Romford. My mum wanted a 'humanist' funeral, which shocked me as I had always thought she was religious, but apparently she didn't believe in God or the afterlife in any shape or form. She told my sister Linda that there was no heaven or hell, and your time on earth was all you [1]. It was a strange funeral. The minister, Keith

Sheperd, was excellent and gave a lovely service. I had written a eulogy about my mum, and due to me not having a proper voice, my sons, Chris, Andy, and Matt, took turns reading different paragraphs from it. They all did a wonderful job, and I was proud of them.

So 2009 ended with the loss of my old Mum, Dot. Such a final thing to know that you will never see that person ever again. You have only got one Mum so that makes her special. I feel very sad that I never got really close to her until the end of her life. She phoned me every day to tell me all her troubles, and as I'm a good listener she enjoyed talking without being interrupted. I'm so pleased that Jackie and I were able to take her to Majorca a year before she died – she loved it and the weather was beautiful. Winston (Jackie's brother) made such a fuss of her – she loved him to bits. Jackie and I got her the best room in the hotel, looking out on the beautiful bay of Palma. Mum sat on her verandah like a queen soaking up the sun and the great view. We took her all round the island through the mountains, ending at Porto Soller where we had a lovely meal at the restaurant by the beach. Her phone number is still on my speed dial on both mobile and home phone, and I just can't bring myself to delete it.

After my Mum's funeral I kept calling on her to visit me in spirit form or show me a sign she was watching over me, but nothing. Maybe she was right that there is no afterlife, but the big question is, 'Where does your spirit go after you die?' Surely it must go somewhere. It gave you life while you were on earth. Surely it doesn't just die with your body like an old battery. Maybe there is a special place where all spirits go. We call it 'Heaven', but it could be just another dimension, as your spirit is invisible to us humans. I can't just believe without some sort of proof. The mystery of life is unknown to us until we pass on ourselves and find out the truth. The only irony is, you can't then come back and tell anyone.

Mum, Dorothy (died on 4th September 2009) RIP

My late brother, John, who was always mad on motorbikes and travelled all over Europe with his wife, Ronnie. He leaves behind his wife and two sons, Steven and David

God bless you John. Rest in Peace.

My sister, Linda, looking happy on holiday

CHAPTER 26

A New Decade – 2010

I hoped this year would be a really good year for everyone and we would all be blessed with good health.

I had started new experimental trials which involved a group of us who had undergone radiotherapy/chemotherapy for cancer to have acupuncture every week for eight weeks, and periodically our saliva was tested to see if the acupuncture had improved it or not. I was in a group of four people: Steve, Diane, Brian and myself. It had been great to talk about our common ailment which is not having much saliva to enable us to eat properly without a drink of water to wash the food down. Also, during the course of the eight weeks, each of us took turns to tell our story of how we battled the cancer. They all agreed that losing your voice box was one of the worst things they could imagine happening to them, and told me that they admired how I coped with it.

Little did they know, I found it very difficult to cope with it, and I put on a front to hide my despair and frustration at having to live as a 'Neckbreather' even though it was two years since my operation. I accepted my situation, but it was very hard to deal with on a day to day basis, especially if I went out in public with my wife, Jackie. I'd try not to speak because people would hear my artificial voice and turn around to stare at me, so I'd get embarrassed for my wife, as people tend to treat me as 'normal' until I open my mouth to speak, and you can see how their attitude changes towards me. It's sad, but it's human nature for people to judge someone like me it seems. They can't help but react in a negative way if you have something different from what would be classed as 'normal'.

It was now the 1st September 2010, three years exactly since I'd had the operation to take away my voice box and vocal chords. They only gave me three months to live, but three years on I was still here. My quality of life wasn't that great, as I yearned to have my old voice back and to be able to sing again.

My passion was always music. It kept me sane going through the bad times, and I so enjoyed singing even though I didn't have the greatest voice. It gave me such joy and pleasure to sing to my backing tracks. I was always singing along with the radio, in the car, any chance I got to sing along to music I would do it. Before my operation I was learning piano so I could one day sing along to my own accompaniment. Sadly that will never happen now. I try not to listen to music now as it's too painful to be reminded how much I have lost and will never have again. My world is now full of silence when I'm on my own. Sometimes two or three hours go by without me speaking, and the phone will ring, and I will pick it up and due to mucus blocking my valve, I'm not able to speak. This happens quite a lot, so I have to put them on hold and clean my valve quickly to be able to speak again.

I do try and talk with this artificial voice through what they call an 'indwelling valve' which allows me to speak in a croaky sounding voice, but it isn't very pleasant to listen to, and after a while of trying to make conversation my wife asks me to stop talking (ha ha). Even I tire of the sound of it, but I practice every day at making it better to the ear and more acceptable to listen too. With technology moving so fast maybe soon someone will invent a new valve 1akes your voice sound wonderful.

Your voice is so important. It's 80 percent of your personality. Just imagine what Tom Jones would do without his precious wonderful voice. He would never have had a career singing and would probably have worked on the building sites as a labourer. Due to his voice, Tom has made millions of dollars, had a fantastic life living the dream that we would all love to, plus Elvis Presley was his best buddy – how cool is that? – all because of his voice. It's amazing how a simple thing like having been blessed with a wonderful singing voice allowed Tom to have all that luxury and riches. So you can see how important your voice is to everyone, and people just take it for granted. When you lose your voice, it affects your whole life and changes your personality forever.

Michael Douglas had been diagnosed with stage four cancer of the throat. He had a tumour at the base of his tongue, the same as I had in 2004. He was having radiotherapy and chemotherapy treatment at the time, and he was positive that he would beat it. My thoughts were with him, as I knew exactly what he is going through. The next few months would be the toughest he had ever faced as the after effects of the treatment are awful, and my heart went out to him and his family. I followed his progress closely. 'Best of luck, Michael. Keep being positive and don't give up.'

At the time of writing, Michael has been given the all clear from cancer and is now leading a normal life again, and has gone back to acting in films once again. Well done, Michael. May you have many more years living cancer-free.

CHAPTER 27

The Man Who Shot the 60s

Mike, Wendy, Jackie and myself were invited to the legendary photographer Duffy's memorial service on Wednesday 22nd September 2010 at St Mary's Church in Chelsea. Duffy sadly passed away on 30th May 2010 from a very debilitating illness in his lungs.

Duffy was the guy who took the famous Cartoone album cover photos, which we will always be proud of forever. He was a genius with a camera and had that gift of capturing the right moment to take a great picture. With Duffy, David Bailey and Donovan, they were known as the 'Black Trinity' as they were so unique in their style and their approach to photography. They brought in a new era where the photographer was even more famous than the models he photographed.

Some of his most famous photos were of Paul McCartney, David Bowie and Charlton Heston, to name just a few of his A-list clients. Plus he also did two Pirelli calendars, and work for *Vogue* and *Elle* magazines.

Brian Duffy – Duffy© Duffy Archive

Jackie and I, plus Mike and Wendy Allison, really enjoyed the service and all the tributes from Duffy's wonderful family. There was a fantastic heartfelt tribute from Lord Puttman who really gave us an insight into the man that was Duffy. Lord Puttman obviously loved and admired Duffy. They were great friends over the years. He talked of many stories about how Brian Duffy could inspire everyone who came in contact with him. Brian had an amazing analytical brain and questioned everything, and took nothing on face value. His favourite saying to his family and nine grandchildren was 'Don't trust anyone's opinion. Find out for yourself. Question everything.'

Chris Duffy has written a book about his dad's life and work. Cartoone are very proud to be included in that book. He is also presenting Duffy exhibitions all over the world to let everyone know about his wonderful talented dad.

Website: www.duffyphotographer.com

Me at the Duffy exhibition with the Cartoone
original album in the case

Jackie and our dear friend, Victoria Rogers-Fertig, and her dog. Victoria passed away in 2015 from a stroke on holiday in the South of France. We didn't know it then, but this was the last time we would see Victoria alive in Brighton. Rest in Peace.

*Mike Allison's birthday party – being presented
with the cake by his daughter, Jaimie.*

Jackie and May Allison (Mike's sister) at his birthday party.

CHAPTER 28

Epilogue

It's 2017 and I still struggle as a laryngectomee. My quality of life is pretty poor really, even after 10 years of living with this disability. I tire of the daily grind of everything I have to do to survive. I can only eat certain foods as I only have a small oesophagus, the size of a straw, and find it difficult to swallow. Because of this, it takes me twice as long to eat as anybody else, and the sound of me swallowing isn't very pleasant, as sometimes I choke, so have to regurgitate my food, which must put people off. So I tend to avoid going out for a meal in a restaurant as it can be very embarrassing for me and the family and friends with me. They are always understanding, but it must be horrible to watch me try to eat. Jackie and I keep in touch with Derek's wife and son, Gwynie and John, also Mike Allison and Wendy, his wife, plus his sister May.

We see them from time to time when our

schedules permit. Gwynie and John did a wonderful thing for all of us, as they both agreed that all the royalties for the Cartoone songs should be split four ways as we all contributed to those songs. We all signed a contract for worldwide publishing with Peter Knight Jr. (Catalyst Music Publishing Ltd). He then got us some royalties which we never got from Atlantic in all those 43 years. We all got £250 each, which I spent on the Cartoone Deluxe Edition CD, and sent it out to as many DJs as I could get hold of to try and promote Cartoone once again.

The only DJs I'm aware of playing any Cartoone tracks are Bob Eberth, Modern Mark, Chris Philips and the late Brian Matthews on his Sound Of The 60s show, who I will be forever grateful to for all their support and faith. Big shout out to Phil Swern who put the show together for Brian Matthews and chose the playlists from the old archives, and wrote the script for the show too.

Chris Philips (BRFM) even did a phone interview with Mike Allison, which was absolutely brilliant. Mike talked about his great friendship with the late Freddy Mercury (Queen) for many years. Freddy was even the publisher of Mike's songs. Also Mike spoke about Cliff Richard and how he wrote half his

DJ – Modern Mark wearing Cartoone T-Shirt

album *I'm Nearly Famous*. When I listened to the show there was a pause when Chris asked Mike if Cartoone had ever played Wales, and when Mike said no Chris was taken aback, but what he didn't realise was that Cartoone never played any gigs in the UK or Europe, which is a shame – we only played the USA.

Joe Reagoso has put the Cartoone Deluxe Edition CD back on his website (www.fridaymusic.com) and it looks great, and I personally am so pleased and grateful for that. We both did a great job of putting together the Cartoone CD which Joe remixed with the extra unreleased tracks I sent him. It was a labour of love as he always loved Cartoone and their music.

I am 70 years old this year, and I certainly feel it, as I find it very difficult to wake up in the morning and have to force myself to get up to start the day. I live for my family as they give me a reason to carry on as long as I possibly can. I ache all over every day, and struggle with being a 'Neckbreather' which is the term used for people like me. After ten years I still can't get used to breathing/coughing through a hole in my neck, rather than my mouth. It is truly a life changing thing to happen to anyone, especially after living 60 years with a good voice, and being able to express myself properly and be understood without having to repeat myself over and over.

The sad thing is that this is as good as it gets I'm afraid, as it won't get better, but it might get worse – that's the worry everyone has to live with. I really try to stay positive and focus on moving forward and trying not to look back. I love Rocky's speech to his son in *Rocky Balboa* – it's absolutely brilliant and so true I think.

I am sitting down most of the time, due to my disability, so I make good use of that by using the computer and teaching myself about website hosting. My son, Andy, and I created a website for the Surrey area: Head & Neck Cancer Support Group (www.secondchancers.co.uk) and it seems to be getting some interest from patients in our catchment area. At least it gives me some purpose in my life towards helping other people like myself.

There is also another website only for laryngectomee's run by Dr. Thomas Moors: www.shoutatcancer.org

Please go and have a look at both sites, as you may find them interesting.

The brilliant dynamic Dr. Thomas Moors, creator and driving force behind laryngectomy charity, Shout At Cancer.

*Shout At Cancer Laryngectomy Choir,
led by Dr Thomas Moors*

President of our Head & Neck Cancer Group,
Patrick Chapman, ENT Surgeon (Retired)

My Jackie and I at 'Stimulate Your Tastebuds' Function in
Lakeside Restaurant, University of Guildford, Surrey

Second Chancers Head & Neck Cancer Support Group, Guildford, Surrey at 'Stimulate Your Tastebuds' event on Tuesday 26th September 2017

Thank you for buying my book, hopefully you have enjoyed reading my story. I wrote it from the heart, and did my best to make it interesting.

Well I don't know what is going to happen in the next few years. Will I still be alive? Who knows? All I do know is that I am going to live in the moment and try not to worry about the future. We only have one life, so we owe it to ourselves to make the best of it.

Life is full of choices, and the people who make the best choices usually have the best life, as good choices are a positive thing, and I have found that positive things do happen to positive people.

Remember, all that matters in life is love as it's the only thing you can take with you when you die. Everything else you have in life you just borrowed for a little while.

CHAPTER 29

A Few People I Have To Mention

JORGE RAMIREZ

There are a few people that I have to mention whom I have met in the last few years since my operation. The first person is my lovely Mexican friend, Jorge Ramirez, who is such a great guy, and who everybody loves (including my family). Jorge is one of those guys who can play any song and make it his own from Spanish Salsa to Reggae right through to Tom Jones and the new song from Rag-N-Bone-Man called 'I'm Only Human' which everybody really enjoys.

Please look up Jorge at his facebook page: www.facebook.com/jorgeramirez058

PAPA GEORGE

The next person I would like to give a mention is the amazingly talented Papa George. He has been awarded a place in the Blues Hall Of Fame in the

USA as a genuine bluesman. This guy is the real deal and he can groove and play the guitar with such 'feel' and technique and sing with his fantastic voice. He has soul and makes any song his own. I have to mention George's wife, Anne, who is a lovely woman and travels everywhere with him.

Please take the time to look him up on his website at: www.papageorge.co.uk (blues with feeling)

ELAINE HARPER

I must mention my dear friend, Elaine Harper, and her lovely family: Ken, Emma, Danae, Andrew and baby Hugo, not forgetting their dog Poppy. Thank you for all your thoughtfulness and kindness always and also for being a constant friend over the many years. You have all been amazing and so supportive. Thank you.

Joyce with her huge car in Philadelphia

JOYCE GREEN

I need to give a big mention to my sister-in-law Joyce Green, who has been struggling with breast cancer for the last five years, and has been told it's terminal. So she is also living on borrowed time. Here is my favourite photo of Joyce when she and her husband, Mark, lived in Philadelphia, and they did something that I always dreamed of.

They drove from one end of the USA (east coast) to San Francisco (west coast) where they set up home for the next four years. What a road trip that must have been. Well done Joyce and family.

I have had an amazing life, full of great memories and adventures. The only thing I would have liked is to have been 'Super Rich' as you can do so much for people if you have loads of money.

RAFAEL NADAL

I read about Rafael Nadal, the tennis player, who comes from Majorca. He booked Disney World for his whole family and paid for it all himself.

Wouldn't that be great to be able to do that for all my family? I would truly love to do that – it would be fantastic.

ANDY MURRAY

I admire my countryman, Andy Murray, who won Wimbledon twice, the last British person to win Wimbledon was Fred Perry 76 years ago. Andy also helped Britain to win the Davis cup and won a Gold Medal at the Olympics. If anyone deserves to be a 'Sir' it's him. Even though he is a bit serious, he is still a great tennis player and an excellent ambassador for Britain.

PAUL CARRACK

'Man With The Golden Voice', Paul Carrack.

Jackie and I have seen him live and he is absolutely fantastic, and we love all his songs.

I also love the fact that he has his son, Jack, on drums for him. It must be so great for Paul to look back onstage and see his son on drums. I bet he is super proud of him. I recommend that you go and see Paul Carrack in concert. Every song is a gem and his performance is phenomenal.

Visit www.paulcarrack.net for more information.

RICHARD DESMOND

Also I would like to give a big shout out to Richard Desmond and his excellent PA, Allison Racher, who has looked after him for years, and is the 'Go-To' person for everything to do with Richard. I have a lot of admiration for Richard and his achievements in everything he does. He makes a success of everything he touches. He has been responsible for making millions of pounds for cancer charities, and obviously has a big heart.

To top it all he is a bloody cool solid drummer, who can turn his hand to any style and play it well.

I take my hat off to you Richard – you certainly are the real deal.

MIKE PERRY

I have to mention my old friend, Mike Perry, who owns Bell Perc in Acton. I have known Mike for 20 years and have seen his business grow from strength to strength. The Bell Perc complex is at

www.bellperc.com for all things drums.

JETT, MARISSA, AND SARAH

The biggest mention has to go out to my lovely daughter-in-laws, Jett, Marissa, and Sarah, who have been amazingly supportive all through my cancer journey. Thank you so much for giving Jackie and I such wonderful, beautiful grandchildren. They are the light of our life and bring us such joy whenever we are around them.

DENISE ROBINS

I am off on holiday for the first time in years. We are going to see Jackie's sister, Denise, who has opened a new Bistro: Annidens Wine Bar Bistro, Tintagel, Cornwall. She told me that she has put special soft foods on the menu just for me (lovely). I'm so looking forward to getting away for a wee holiday.

SECOND CHANCERS HEAD & NECK CANCER SUPPORT GROUP

Must give a shout out to the Second Chancers Head & Neck Cancer Support Group. Enthusiastically driven by our President, Patrick Chapman, retired ENT Surgeon. Supported by myself and my wife, Jackie, plus other members of the committee, Lisa Pitkin, Mariana Gaulton, Sandra Levinge, Ann Hope, Margaret Faultless, Jan Humphries, Lucy McGill, Robert Flavell, Dave Stanford, Mike Pendrell and Mary Pinn, who support the many patients and families in the Surrey area.

GEORGE BENSON

I can't possibly leave out the man who has been the soundtrack to my life over the last 40 years; the wonderful and amazing George Benson who is my favourite singer/guitarist of all time. He is still touring and giving pleasure to millions of people in the world. Visit his website for more info: www.georgebenson.com

WHIPLASH (FILM)

Must end this chapter by mentioning my favourite film at the moment. I watched the DVD at home. It's called *Whiplash* and it's about a young drummer who is really dedicated and wants to be the best he can be. In my opinion it's definitely a classic drumming film I urge anyone who loves music to see. It stars Miles Teller as Andrew, the young drummer, and JK Simmons as his very strict and exacting mentor. The acting is superb, and JK got the Oscar for Best Supporting Actor, and I think that Miles should have got Best Actor for his performance which was awesome and very inspiring. The story is brilliant, and draws you in till you become engrossed in the film and end up willing him to do well. This is a must-see for every drummer.

CHAPTER 30

Where Are They Now?

FLETCHER

In May 2005 Fletcher released a video of their song 'Throwaway' from their debut CD *My Revenge*. It's on YouTube (just search 'Fletcher –Throwaway' and click on the Deck Cheese version). It's brilliant in my opinion and really shows how good the band were live.

Sadly, Fletcher split up on 17th July 2005 and played their last gig at the London Barfly.

Sad, as they were a bloody good live band. www. myspace.com/fletcherpunkuk is their website for as long as it stays up there. I still think *My Revenge* is a great CD which deserved more exposure than it got.

HAMISH STUART

Hamish has his own record company called Sulphuric Records and released his own solo CDs *Sooner Or Later* and the brilliant *Real Live*, recorded at the famous 606 jazz club with his band The Hamish Stuart Band, which included Ian Thomas (drums), Adam Philips (lead guitar), and Steve Pearce (bass). He also plays in another band called JimJam with Jim Mullen (guitar), Ian Thomas (drums), Graham Harvey (keyboards), and Pino Paladino (bass). They released an excellent CD in 2002 and are due to release the follow up soon. Hamish has his own site at:

www.sulphuricrecords.co.uk for all things Hamish.

He also has a new band called 360 featuring Hamish, Steve Ferrone, and Molly Duncan from the Average White Band. The new CD is brilliant and definitely worth buying in my opinion. You can reach them on their facebook page:

www.facebook.com/360bandofficial

MIKE ALLISON

Mike has proved the most successful of all the Cartoone members. He has won a Grammy for a song written by him for Olivia Newton-John called 'Every Face Tells A Story' – a number one record in the charts here and the USA. This song was also sung by Cliff Richard, plus Mike wrote half the songs on Cliff's album, *I'm Nearly Famous*. He owns a recording studio in London, and develops young up and coming artists. He also has his own publishing company. Lately, he has been producing Andy Bell (Erasure) and is doing fantastic. He is also writing musicals as another string to his bow (is there no end to this man's talent?) Well done Mike! Best of luck to you mate. You deserve all the success that you've earned by all your hard work and talent. You couldn't have done it without the lovely Wendy, your very clever and supportive wife.

MARK LONDON

Mark is still writing and producing music, but doesn't manage bands since the demise of Stone The Crows after Leslie's death in 1972. The band lasted another year, but it was never the same, as Leslie was the main link in the band along with singer Maggie Bell. The band folded in 1973 and Maggie released a brilliant solo album: *Queen Of The Night* with Steve Gadd on drums, which did really well in the states reaching number ten in the charts. Mark produced her second album *Suicide Sal* which didn't sell as well as *Queen*, but Maggie managed to tour the USA and Europe before slowing down and writing music for Films and TV. Her most famous song featured in the show *Taggart*. I believe she now lives in London, and has a band with old drummer from Stone The Crows, Colin Allen, and Zoot Money on keyboards. I read that Mark has won an award for best song in the Canadian Hall Of Fame for his brilliant classic song 'To Sir With Love'. Well done Mark. It's a fantastic song that will live on forever.

LULU

Since I last saw Lulu in 1969, she has divorced Maurice and married her hairdresser, John Freida, who used to cut my hair back in the day when I had some hair to cut and is now world famous for his salons and hair products. They have a son together, Jordan, who is now an actor. Lulu divorced John in 1991 and began to concentrate on her solo career, and in 1997 she released a fantastic CD called *Independence*, and also got another number one with boy band Take That with the single 'Relight My Fire'. Then on the 20th May 2002 she released a duets style CD which was called *Together*. It got to number four in the charts the first week it came out – not bad eh? I have heard 'Take Me Where The Poor Boys Dance' which was written by Lulu and her brother, Billy Lawrie, plus another person. In my opinion, it's the best thing she has ever done. Lulu released her new book about her life called *I Don't Wanna Fight*, which is an enjoyable read that I can recommend. It reads like a novel rather than a biography.

Lulu is still touring the UK and enjoying every minute of it. I read that she enjoys it even more as time has gone by, as she appreciates how great it is to be still performing with her excellent band to a live audience to sold-out gigs – very exciting indeed. It's amazing how Lulu still gives it 100 percent on stage. She never ceases to be the best that she can be every night on tour.

www.luluofficial.com

There's a great Cartoone website run by Tom McCartney called www.rockingscots.co.uk which is not only a wonderful webpage all about Cartoone (with photos) but also has loads of other 60s Scottish bands featured too. Go have a look as it's a brilliant site.

I have started a new webpage on myspace in memory of my old band Cartoone and also Derek Creigan and Mo Trowers who both have sadly passed away. I put a short story about the band, Derek and Mo, and also our music is up there too. So far we have had loads of plays and rising. There are 64 million people on myspace, so if 10 million listen to Cartoone and hear Derek's unique voice, wouldn't that be wonderful.

www.myspace.com/cartoone
A tribute to Derek and Mo.
Cartoone Facebook Page:
www.facebook.com/ScottishBandCartoone

AHMET M. ERTEGUN (Atlantic Records)

The Legendary Ahmet Ertegun sadly passed away at the age of 83 years. After an accidental fall at a Rolling Stones concert in New York in October 2006, he had been in a coma, and died on 14th December 2006 with his family at his bedside.

Ahmet was the founder of the famous Atlantic Records in 1947, and with Jerry Wexler and the great engineer, Tom Dowd, discovered artists like Aretha Franklin, Ray Charles, Buffalo Spingfield, The Rascals, Phil Collins, The Rolling Stones and Average White Band to name just a few.

In 1968, Ahmet and Jerry signed both Cartoone and Led Zeppelin to Atlantic Records. Both bands released debut albums in the USA and toured together in 1969. Jimmy Page was guest artist on Cartoone's album playing guitar with them, basically in session man mode.

I was lucky enough to have lunch with Ahmet in his Atlantic Records Chairman's office in New York on the 9th June 2003. He was gracious and funny and we talked about the old Atlantic days when the bands meant something to the record companies and they believed in them. He told me some wonderful stories about the old days. What a special day that was for me. The sun was shining in New York and I was staying in a really nice hotel, plus I was having lunch with the legendary Ahmet Ertegun. How cool is that? Ahmet Ertegun will be sorely missed, as he was respected and loved by musicians all over the planet, and his legacy will stand the test of time.

His personality and warmth, and his business sense, gave him a unique quality which made Ahmet so special, and he thoroughly deserves the accolade of being called a 'Legend'. Ahmet still kept in touch with many musicians that were signed to his label. That was the special character he had and that's why everyone loved him.

There was a memorial service in New York to celebrate this wonderful man's life. I wasn't asked to go, as I wasn't famous enough. Eric Clapton, Mick Jagger, Jimmy Page, Robert Plant, Phil Collins and Tony Bennet were some of the artists who were invited to this great man's memorial service. If there is such a place as heaven, Ahmet will be joining all his artists, like Ray Charles, Otis Redding, Maurice Gibb, Robin Gibb, Derek Creigan and Mo Trowers, who have sadly passed away. I'm sure he will be having a ball up there, as music was his life.

There will only ever be one Ahmet Ertegun. They broke the mould after him.

LESLIE HARVEY

Leslie died in a tragic accident at the Top Rank Ballroom in Swanage on the 3rd May 1972. He was electrocuted on stage as he moved forward with his guitar and touched the microphone to announce the band. He had so much talent as a brilliant guitarist and songwriter with his band Stone The Crows – such a tragic waste. The world is a poorer place without him and his guitar. He will never be forgotten by his friends and fans or myself.

Just sharing the stage and watching him play every night on tour in the USA was awesome and an honour to witness. To see him get standing ovations nearly every night was a joy to behold, and a privilege to be a part of.

Rest in Peace Leslie, my old friend and band mate.

DEREK CREIGAN

Derek died suddenly after an operation for a brain tumor. Sadly, Derek didn't fulfill his lifelong ambition to get a number one record in the charts. On reflection, I think a few of Cartoone's songs, especially on the second album, deserved to be given an opportunity and recorded by some of the pop stars of today. Wouldn't it have been nice for Derek to have a posthumous number one?

The Cartoone songs were brilliant and very emotionally thought provoking. If it wasn't for Derek and his very distinctive voice and style, we would never have met Mark London, or been signed by Atlantic Records, or toured the USA with Led Zeppelin So Derek and Cartoone have achieved what millions of bands will never achieve – that's something to be proud of isn't it.

Thanks a million Derek. May you find everlasting peace.

JOHN CREIGAN (DRUMMER)

John is Derek and Gwynie's son and he has grown up to be really tall like his Dad. He is a lovely guy who Derek would have been proud of.

John is very proud of his Dad and is a big fan of Cartoone and loves their music.

John has joined a band in Brighton and they have released lots of music. It's such a pity Derek is not around to see his son play drums with his band Grand Parade – it would have been wonderful.

Wishing you every success John. Best of luck in all that you do.

Have a wee look at their website:
www.grandparade.bandcamp.com

MAURICE GIBB

The bass player/vocalist of the world famous BeeGees died suddenly on Sunday 12th January 2003 at the age of 53 years. He was taken into hospital after he had stomach pains on Wednesday 8th, and at 4am on Thursday 9th he had a massive cardiac arrest. The surgeons decided to operate after they resuscitated him due to a twisted intestine which apparently he'd had from birth. Maurice never really fully regained consciousness and passed away on Sunday. Barry and Robin, his brothers, and fellow BeeGees decided to have the funeral in Florida where Maurice has lived with his family for the last 30 years. Lulu divorced him in 1973 and Maurice met and married Yvonne in 1982. They have two children Adam (26) and Samantha (22). The world will be a sadder place without Maurice:

a wonderful kind, caring, and generous person, and a great friend to me. I will never forget you.

MO TROWERS

I was shocked and stunned to have just heard from Mo's family that he had sadly passed away in Australia in 2004 from natural causes. Mo was my best pal, and was like a big brother to me. We shared many flats together over the Chevlons/Cartoone years. The last flat was in

Gloucester Rd, London in 1969. He introduced me to music from Ray Charles, Aretha Franklin, Solomon Burke, Marvin Gaye and all the Tamla family, to name a few.

It was Mo that taught me how the 'feel' or 'groove' of a song gave it the magic and brought it to life. Mo was a brilliant rhythm guitarist, with an amazing knack of getting just the right tempo or groove that suited the song. He was an important part of the Cartoone sound, and provided that steady rock solid rhythm behind the drums and the bass. Also, his excellent backing vocals were an integral part of the four-part harmony that Cartoone used.

Many a night we'd sit up late and study how songs were put together and analyse how each instrument affected the other. It was a science to him. I think people didn't give him credit for his vast understanding and knowledge of music. We would practice for hours trying to learn our craft and emulate our musical heroes of the 1960s.

Mo was always kind and thoughtful, with a friendly smile for everyone he met. He gave his time freely and always encouraged other musicians he met. Mo was a special man with high principals and a code that he lived by, which would make anyone who knew him feel proud that they did. I feel sad that he never had any children, as he would have been a wonderful Dad. Pity we lost touch when he went to Australia around 15 years ago. Mo's lost years – it's a mystery what happened to him over there in Australia.

God bless you Mo, and thank you for your friendship. If there is such a place as Heaven, then you deserve to be there, and I hope there is a great band for you to play in.

DENNIS SHEEHAN

Dennis was Cartoone's tour manager from 1968 to 1969, and he organized their tour of the USA in 1969 supporting Led Zeppelin and other world-class bands. Everything went like clockwork with Dennis at the helm. No wonder he became such a legend with Led Zeppelin and U2 over the years.

Dennis sadly passed away from a massive heart attack in a Los Angeles on Wednesday 27th May 2015.

I have known Dennis since the Cartoone days, and I lived with him and his then wife, Lisa, in his house for about a year. Then he began tour managing for Stone The Crows. He always kept in touch over the years, which shows the measure of the man. Bono wrote a glowing tribute on U2's website to the irreplaceable man which Dennis was. A unique person who I loved and will always remember.

God bless you Dennis – Rest in Peace.

MARION MASSEY

Marion Massey became one of the first female music managers in the 1960s. She discovered Lulu (Marie Mcdonald McLaughlin Lawrie) aged 14 at the Lindella Club (a Glasgow discotheque), became her manager/mentor and changed her name to Lulu. She managed her very successfully for 25 years. Marion also co-managed Cartoone with Mark London and Peter Grant from 1967 to 1969 when they split up after being dropped by Atlantic Records. I will always remember Marion as a really kind and very intelligent woman who treated me with genuine warmth and affection. Thank you for the two years you looked after Cartoone and me. You were the best – a great person and manager.

Marion sadly died in London on 1st March 2014. I hope there is such a place as Heaven as I'm sure you will be there. God bless you Marion.

JOHN BONHAM

John Bonham died in 1975 at Jimmy Page's house after a night of heavy drinking. No one heard anything until they discovered John in the morning. So tragic, especially for someone who was so talented and thought of as 'the world's best drummer' at the time. I, for one, thought that he was the most amazing and imaginative drummer I have ever seen. He had a fire and a certain something that all great artists have – this is what makes them special. He will be missed by me and so many fans who loved him dearly. I am so proud to have shared the stage with him in the USA.

You are and always will be The Best Of The Best. Rest in Peace John.

JOHN PAUL JONES

John is still out there recording and playing live, also writing and producing for other bands.

www.johnpauljones.com

ROBERT PLANT

Robert has just released a new album called *Carry Fire* with his band The Sensational Space Shifters which, in my opinion, is one of the best he has done in a long time. His tour is sold out already. Well done Robert for keeping the flame burning, and your music legacy alive.

www.robertplant.com

JIMMY PAGE

I don't know what Jimmy is up to at the moment: he never calls and never writes (joking). I haven't seen Jimmy since we last played with Zeppelin in 1969. I feel privileged to have known the legendary Jimmy Page and to have shared the stage in the USA and an album (*Cartoone*) with him. Please take a look at his website for everything Jimmy Page.

www.jimmypage.com

Our Lovely New Dog

Darling little DAISY